WHAT'S THE DEAL?

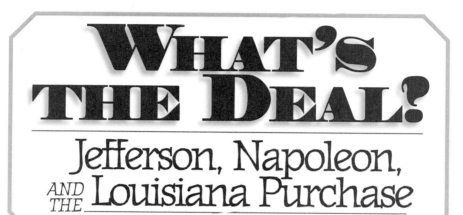

WHAT'S THE DEAL?

Jefferson, Napoleon, AND THE Louisiana Purchase

by Rhoda Blumberg

SCHOLASTIC INC.

New York Toronto London Auckland Sydney
Mexico City New Delhi Hong Kong

I am grateful to Barbara Lalicki, ideal editor, whose dedication and talents always improve the quality of my work. I am also indebted to James P. Ronda, H. G. Barnard Professor of Western American History, University of Tulsa, who scrutinized my manuscript for accuracy and assisted me with his expert advice. I thank the librarians at the Croton Free Library, the White Plains Library, and the Center for the Humanities, in New York City, for helping me search for and find primary sources.

The frontispiece artwork was created for this book by John Buxton. Maps from the National Geographic Society's cartographic database were customized for this book by Carl Mehler, Senior Map Editor, and Joe Ochlak, Map Researcher.

For information regarding permission, write to National Geographic Society, 1145 17th Street, NW, Washington, DC 20036.

0-439-12920-6

Published by Scholastic Inc., 555 Broadway, New York, NY 10012, by arrangement with National Geographic Society.

SCHOLASTIC and associated logos are trademarks and/or registered trademarks of Scholastic Inc.

12 11 10 9 8 7 6 5 4 3 2   9/9 0 1 2 3 4/0

Printed in the U.S.A.   40

First Scholastic printing, September 1999

For my sister,
Cynthia

Table of Contents

Cast of Characters

The Discoverer

La Salle, René-Robert Cavelier

In 1682 this French explorer claimed a vast territory both east and west of the Mississippi River that stretched from Canada in the north to the Gulf of Mexico in the south. He named it Louisiana to honor his King, Louis XIV.

The Leading Players

Adams, John

Vice President under President Washington (1789–1797), he served as President from 1797 to 1801. His presidency was marked by the crisis of an undeclared war, the quasi war, with France. Adams was defeated by Thomas Jefferson in the presidential race of 1800.

Bonaparte, Napoleon

As a French Army officer, his victories in Italy and Austria helped him rise to power during the French Revolution. On November 9, 1799, he seized control of the government and made himself First Consul with more power than any king. In 1802 he proclaimed himself dictator for life.

Jefferson, Thomas

Author of the Declaration of Independence, he became America's Minister to France (1785–1789), President Washington's Secretary of State (1790–1793), President Adams's Vice President (1797–1801), and President (1801–1809). Jefferson was the leader of the pro-French, anti-British Republican Party.

Livingston, Robert R.

Member of the Continental Congress, he helped draft the Declaration of Independence. Appointed by President Jefferson to be Minister to France (1801–1804), he and James Monroe negotiated the Louisiana Purchase Treaty.

Monroe, James

This patriot had been a U.S. Senator (1790–1794), Minister to France (1794–1796), and Governor of Virginia (1799–1802) before being chosen Envoy Extraordinary to France by President Jefferson (1803). There he assisted Livingston in negotiations that resulted in the Louisiana Purchase Treaty. He succeeded James Madison as President of the United States (1817–1825).

Toussaint L'Ouverture

Leader of a slave rebellion in the French Caribbean colony of St. Domingue (now Haiti), he became dictator of the island (1801) and leader of the army that defeated Napoleon's troops in 1802. Napoleon had him kidnapped and imprisoned in the French Alps, where he died in 1803.

The Kings

Louis XIV (1643–1715)

Called the Sun King because of his extravagance, he imposed absolute rule over France. His grand palace at Versailles was more important to him than the land La Salle had named for him in North America.

Louis XV (1715–1774)

Even though Louisiana was many times the size of France, he considered it valueless and gave it away to Spain in 1762.

Louis XVI (1774–1792)

He and his wife, Queen Marie Antoinette, were guillotined in 1793 during the French Revolution.

SPAIN

Charles III (1759–1788)

He received Louisiana as a "gift" from his cousin, France's King Louis XV, in 1762. His hostility toward England later led this king to support the American Revolution.

Charles IV (1788–1808)

This ineffectual King gave Louisiana to France by a secret treaty in 1800. In return, Napoleon was supposed to give a kingdom in northern Italy to the King's daughter Luisetta.

ENGLAND

George III (1760–1820)

Remembered as the King who lost the American Colonies, he threatened to attack the fleet Napoleon planned to send to New Orleans.

The Queen

Maria Luisa, Queen of Spain and the overbearing wife of King Charles IV, dominated negotiations that resulted in the transfer of Louisiana to Napoleon by a secret treaty in 1800.

The Spies

Genêt, Edmond Charles Éduoard

Minister to the U.S. from France (1793–1794), he recruited Americans to help with his planned invasion of Spanish Louisiana.

Wilkinson, James

Known as Agent Number 13, this American was paid by Spain to spy against the United States (1787–1803 or 1804). For part of this time Wilkinson was in command of the United States Army (1796–1812). In 1805 he became Governor of Louisiana Territory.

Other Players

FRANCE

Barbé-Marbois, François de

As Minister of Finance under Napoleon, he negotiated the sale of Louisiana to the United States.

Bonaparte, Joseph and Lucien

Two of Napoleon's four brothers, they were opposed to the sale of Louisiana to the United States.

Bonaparte, Josephine

Napoleon was passionately in love with this woman, whom he married in 1796.

Bonaparte, Pauline

One of Napoleon's three sisters, she was married to General Leclerc.

Leclerc, Charles Victor Emmanuel

Brother-in-law of Napoleon, he was sent to St. Domingue (1801) to defeat Toussaint L'Ouverture and his army of ex-slaves. Instead, he and thousands of his troops died there of yellow fever.

Talleyrand, Charles Maurice de

This charming, clever, cunning, corrupt diplomat was Napoleon's Minister of Foreign Affairs from 1799 to 1807.

SPAIN

Gálvez, Bernardo de

While Governor of Spanish Louisiana (1777–1783), he led armed forces to aid the rebellious American Colonies against England.

Morales, Juan Ventura

In 1802 this Spanish administrator closed the port of New Orleans to United States shipping.

ENGLAND

Baring, Alexander

Representing Baring & Co., a family banking business, he arranged to finance the sale of Louisiana to the United States.

UNITED STATES

Hamilton, Alexander

As President Washington's Secretary of the Treasury (1789–1795), he persuaded the President to adopt a policy of neutrality. Hamilton headed the pro-British, anti-French Federalist Party.

Jay, John

This New York politician, who favored the interests of eastern commerce, negotiated a treaty with the British in 1794. Its anti-French bias created such commotion that the country became divided into two political parties—the pro-British Federalists and the pro-French Republicans.

Madison, James

Instrumental in drawing up the Constitution's Bill of Rights, this patriot was "second-in-command" of the Republican Party, which was headed by Jefferson. He was Jefferson's Secretary of State (1801–1809) and succeeded him as President (1809–1817).

Pinckney, Charles
Gerry, Elbridge
Marshall, John

Appointed by President Adams, these men traveled to France in 1797 to negotiate an end to the quasi war between the United States and France and became involved in the XYZ Affair.

Pinckney, Thomas

As Special Commissioner to Spain (1795–1796), he negotiated the Pinckney Treaty, which guaranteed the United States navigation rights on the Lower Mississippi River and made New Orleans a duty-free port.

Washington, George

"Father of our Country," he was Commander of the Continental Armies (1779–1783) and first President of the United States (1789–1797). To keep America out of wars with foreign powers, he issued a proclamation of neutrality in 1793.

1 Napoleon Eyes North America

IN 1800 NAPOLEON BONAPARTE RULED FRANCE as a dictator with powers that none dared challenge. After commanding a series of triumphant military campaigns in Italy and Austria, he had become France's hero. And when he used force to grab control of the government on November 9, 1799, he was acclaimed as an ideal ruler who had ended the ten-year turmoil of the French Revolution.

During that revolution King Louis XVI, his Queen, Marie Antoinette, and thousands of aristocrats were beheaded by the guillotine. Many nobles, including the conniving politician Talleyrand, fled to the new United States of America, seeking safety in exile. Some returned to France as soon as they could.

Their country's new ruler had boundless ambition. In earlier times, a French king had given the province of Louisiana in America to Spain. Like many in France, Napoleon saw this as a crime committed by royalty against the French people.

He was determined to get it back.

NAPOLEON HAD AMBITIONS to cross the Atlantic and establish an empire in North America.
Below: Thousands of people were beheaded by the guillotine during the French Revolution.

French Louisiana

LA SALLE PLANTED *a cross at the mouth of the Mississippi River and claimed land he called Louisiana for France.*
Below: His King, Louis XIV, didn't want the territory.

The land called Louisiana had been claimed and named in 1682 by the French explorer La Salle to honor King Louis XIV. Planting a cross at the mouth of the Mississippi River, he proclaimed: "I . . . do now take, in the name of His Majesty and of his successors to the crown, possession of this country of Louisiana, its seas, harbors, ports, bays, adjacent straits, and all the nations, peoples [Native Americans] . . . mines, minerals, fisheries, streams, and rivers."[1] Louisiana consisted of immense expanses of wilderness east and west of the Mississippi River that stretched from Canada in the north to the Gulf of Mexico in the south.

The glorious Sun King, Louis XIV, was not impressed with his new province. He considered this new acquisition "quite useless" and was not interested in colonizing it. His Majesty was more concerned about constructing a palace at Versailles and fighting a war against Spain.[2]

It was not until 1699 that French colonists began to settle in

Louisiana. They were sponsored by investors of a private company interested in land speculation. King Louis XIV had given his approval to their Louisiana Company so that settlers and soldiers could immigrate " . . . in order to hinder the English from taking possession there."[3] Several hundred people purchased land they assumed was fertile for farming or profitable for mining gold and silver, and left France to settle in the New World.

Over the years, most immigrants made their homes in or near New Orleans. Some chose to establish themselves in villages along the Mississippi. Many French fur trappers, Indian traders, boatmen, and farmers came from Canada to Upper Louisiana (north of present-day St. Louis). But most of this tremendous territory remained unexplored and unknown to all but the original occupants—Native Americans.

FRENCH LOUISIANA was an enormous territory that included the Mississippi River and all of its tributaries.

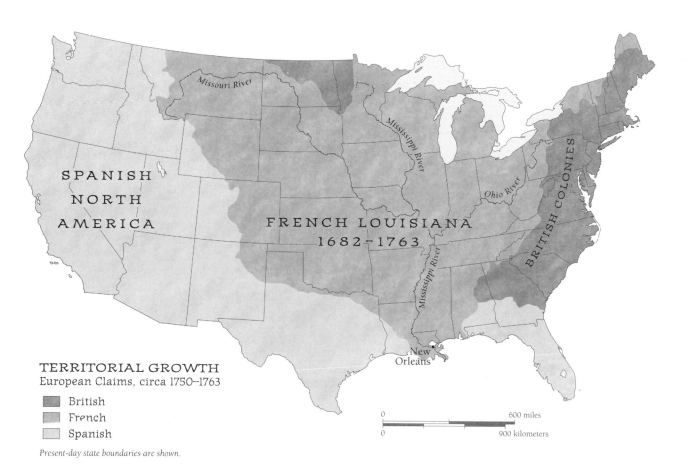

TERRITORIAL GROWTH
European Claims, circa 1750–1763

British
French
Spanish

Present-day state boundaries are shown.

TWO FUR TRAPPERS *prepare to catch beavers in the Louisiana wilderness.*

The French and Indian War

By the 1750s only a few thousand French people could be found in the Louisiana territory, but France was still a powerful force in North America. From 1754 to 1763 it fought England for control of the continent in the French and Indian War.

When England proved victorious, France's chance to rule the New World was destroyed. The British took Canada and all French territory east of the Mississippi River, down to the Gulf of Mexico. The conquerors didn't bother taking the part of Louisiana that was west of the great river. They viewed it as worthless wilderness.

A Royal Gift

Disgusted by defeat and disenchanted by prospects of wealth from North America, France's King Louis XV decided to get rid of Louisiana. Even though the area was many times the size of

FRANCE, SPAIN, AND ENGLAND *all had colonies in the Caribbean. At one time or another, all three ruled Dominica, pictured below.*

France, His Royal Highness didn't want it because most of the land was uncharted wilderness. It could never compare in value with France's wealthy Caribbean colony, St. Domingue (now Haiti). It was France's proudest possession and one of the world's richest colonies. Most French overseas investments were there. The colony was said to have been the source of one-third of France's wealth. Each year, hundreds of ships carried profitable cargoes of sugar, indigo, and other produce from there to France. St. Domingue generated riches for many French people, and King Louis XV deemed it to be far more valuable than any land on the continent of North America.

The French King, therefore, presented Louisiana to his cousin, Charles III of Spain. Pretending to be big-hearted, Louis XV stated that he was rewarding Spain for its help in fighting the British in the French and Indian War. He did apologize to his royal cousin for such a measly gift by writing to him, "I realize that Louisiana indemnifies Your Majesty only slightly" and could not make up for losses in battle.[4]

At first, Spain's King refused to accept this gigantic part of North America. As France's ally, Spain had lost the Floridas to England. King Charles III thought Louisiana was miserable compensation for his country's loss. However, Spain's ministers feared that if the Spanish didn't accept it, England would grab it. Then British soldiers would be near Spain's priceless silver mines in Mexico—too close for comfort. There was another good reason for taking Louisiana. It included New Orleans, the port that controlled Mississippi River traffic.

Ministers in Madrid prevailed upon their King to take the territory. And so, according to a separate, secret agreement in 1762 that preceded the final peace treaty of 1763, Louis XV gave "all of the country known as Louisiana" to Spain. This consisted of New Orleans and land west of the Mississippi.[5]

That France no longer owned an inch of territory on the North American continent did not concern His Majesty in Paris.

2 Spanish Louisiana

KING CHARLES III OF SPAIN was so indifferent to his gift from France that he didn't bother to send officials and soldiers to control his new land. Because French administrators continued to rule the territory, settlers didn't know about the change of government for two years. Then a letter arrived from King Louis XV in 1764 stating that Spanish dons were to become their rulers.

French people living in New Orleans sent representatives to Paris to protest the changeover. Perhaps they believed that their appeals had been successful, because Spanish officials didn't show up. They would have been horrified to hear that King Louis XV actually reassured Charles III that France would never take back Louisiana.

DON ANTONIO DE ULLOA was the first governor of Spanish Louisiana. Right: Spanish warships could be seen at the port of New Orleans.

Protestors

Four years after the secret agreement, in 1766, Don Antonio de Ulloa arrived in New Orleans to begin Spanish rule. He was so unpopular that mobs marched through the streets of New Orleans protesting his presence. Ulloa fled from Louisiana, fearing for his life. He was replaced by General Alexander O'Reilly, a

despotic military governor known as "Bloody" O'Reilly. This fearsome official sentenced five protestors to death and threatened to imprison anyone who refused to pledge allegiance to Spain.

Much to everyone's relief, Don Luis de Unzaga, a mild-mannered man, took over after "Bloody" O'Reilly departed in 1770. The new governor enjoyed the company of Frenchmen, and appointed many of them to help run the government. Even though most of the people in Louisiana were French, spoke French, and followed French customs, Unzaga was so well liked that he helped reconcile them to a Spanish government.

French culture dominated, but Spain ruled.

The British Menace

Before the American Revolution, Spanish Louisiana's most terrifying enemy was just across the Mississippi. England owned the east side of the river. There the British installed ports, built forts, founded towns, and farmed the land. They dominated the Lower Mississippi. One of the port towns—Baton Rouge, a port less than 80 miles from New Orleans—was guarded by fortifications that showed British strength.

According to Spanish law, British traders were forbidden to enter Louisiana. However, this law was ineffective. There just wasn't enough money or military strength to enforce it.

British traders captured most of Louisiana's business. British agents set up headquarters in New Orleans to spy, smuggle goods, sell produce, and incite Indians against Spaniards. British sloops sailed down the river carrying furs from Indian trappers and produce from their own farmers. British boats, called floating stores, could easily be found on the river selling food and supplies to people in New Orleans and to villages along the west side of the river.

Spanish officials were frustrated. They knew their people were dependent upon the British for much of their food.

SPANISH DONS, *men of wealth and title, held positions of power in New Orleans.*

Helping American Rebels

When the American Revolution started in 1775, Louisiana's Governor, Don Luis de Unzaga, received a letter from General Charles Lee of the rebellious American Colonies appealing for help. Lee warned that if England won, British soldiers would then attack Spain's most precious holdings, Mexico and Cuba. General Lee emphasized that an independent America would never attack territory claimed by Spain.

Governor Unzaga decided to aid America's rebels secretly, for he feared that if England found out he was helping them, the British Navy would attack New Orleans.

In June 1779, when it seemed certain that American Revolutionary forces were conquering the British, the Spanish government became bold enough to declare open war against England. Bernardo de Gálvez, Louisiana's Governor at this time, led Spanish soldiers, Indian warriors, and volunteers in battle. He successfully attacked British strongholds on the banks of the Mississippi and along the shores of the Gulf of Mexico.

France also helped the Americans win their War of Independence. Besides furnishing armaments and financial aid, it sent thousands of soldiers to fight side by side with the rebellious colonists and dispatched ships to attack British vessels. France was not concerned about acquiring territory in North America at the time. Its goal was weakening its enemy, England.

BERNARDO DE GÁLVEZ,
Spanish Louisiana's Governor during the American Revolution, helped fight the British.

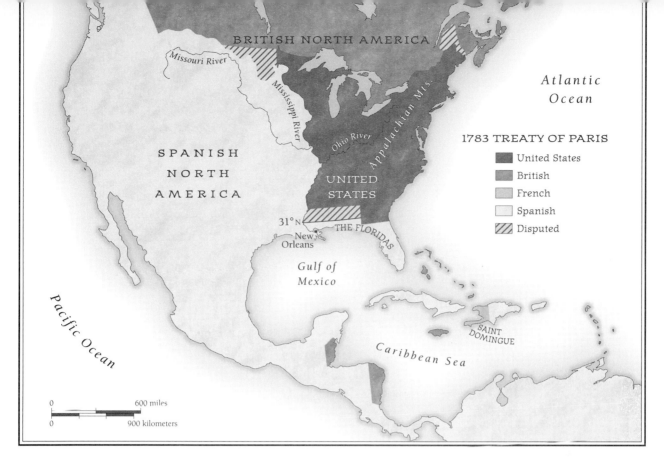

The 1783 Treaty of Paris

When the American Revolutionary War ended with the 1783 Treaty of Paris, a defeated England gave the United States all lands south of Canada, north of the Floridas, and east of the Mississippi. This river became the boundary between Spanish Louisiana and the new, independent American Republic. Even though Spain officially governed the river, the treaty specified that "the navigation of the river Mississippi, from its source to the ocean, shall remain forever free and open to . . . the citizens of the United States."[1]

All things considered, His Majesty Charles III and his subjects were delighted with the treaty. They got back the Floridas from England. Spain controlled the Gulf of Mexico's shores and claimed the east side of the Mississippi as far north as the Ohio River. [2]

Spanish elation evaporated when it became apparent that the United States, whose independence Spain had helped to bring about, had replaced England as a country to fear.

THIS MAP SHOWS TERRITORIAL *claims after the signing of the 1783 Treaty of Paris that ended the Revolutionary War. France no longer controlled land on the continent of North America.*

3 American Settlers

BEFORE THE REVOLUTION only a few American settlers had ventured beyond the Appalachian Mountains. After the peace treaty, an astounding number of Americans headed West. Most of them were farmers, but hunters, traders, and adventurers also came in droves. Some who claimed lands along the banks of the Upper Mississippi pushed across what is now Ohio, Indiana, and Illinois before settling in Spanish Louisiana. Others, from Virginia, Georgia, and other southern states, headed for Kentucky and Tennessee, where they cleared the land, grew crops, made whiskey, and raised cattle.

DANIEL BOONE HEADS WEST *with a band of settlers in 1775. Below: Villages like Ste. Genevieve, founded by the French, flourished along the banks of the Mississippi.*

The Mississippi River was their highway of commerce. They exported their products through New Orleans, across the Gulf of Mexico to various Atlantic ports.

The arrival of large numbers of newcomers angered Spaniards in Louisiana. They declared that Americans were intruders. They also insisted that they alone ruled Mississippi River traffic. In 1784, to stop the growth of American settlements, the Spanish closed the Lower Mississippi to foreigners.

This violated the terms of the 1783 Treaty

FLATBOATS LIKE THIS ONE *were used to carry goods down the Mississippi River.*

of Paris that guaranteed Americans rights to the river.

American settlers were enraged. Only rough trails over mountains and through dense forests connected them with the East. Therefore, they relied on the Mississippi River to ship their produce down to New Orleans, then out to Atlantic ports.

Closing access to this important harbor would ruin farmers, fur trappers, traders, and boatmen. A few thought about becoming citizens of Spanish Louisiana so that they could use the river freely. Some plotted to secede from the Union and form their own nation. Others demanded that Congress insist that Spain reopen the river. Extremists urged the United States to send troops, invade the entire Mississippi Valley, and occupy New Orleans.

Opponents of Western Expansion

Easterners were not disturbed by the closing of the Mississippi, and quite a few were frankly delighted. They opposed an expanded America because it would weaken their own political

32

power. Most eastern merchants did not expect to profit from western expansion, and they didn't want new lands to lure people away from their workshops, stores, and banks.

Commerce from the Atlantic coastline was their concern, not trade and traffic in faraway settlements.

Hoping to please Americans who were opposed to western expansion, Congress appointed Secretary of Foreign Affairs John Jay to negotiate a treaty with Spain.

Jay was a New York politician biased in favor of eastern merchants and shipowners. He did not voice objections to Spain's closing the river to American traffic. Instead, he proposed that Americans be allowed to send ships from their Atlantic coastal ports to trade in Spain. In exchange for this privilege, which favored Easterners, the Spanish would have complete control of Mississippi River traffic for 25 to 30 years.

This angered frontiersmen and people like Thomas Jefferson who looked eagerly toward westward expansion. Jefferson was in France transacting treaties for the United States with foreign countries, but he played no part in negotiating agreements with Spain. When he learned about the proposed Jay Treaty with Spain, he denounced it as an "infamous act . . . against the legislature and the people of the U.S."[1] His friend James Madison, who was in Virginia at the time, echoed this concern. He exclaimed, "The use of the Mississippi is given by nature to our western country, and no power on earth can take it from them."[2]

Violent opposition and threats that Westerners would join Spain or ask England's aid to regain use of the river helped block Jay's proposed treaty. It was never ratified by Congress.

Jay's actions showed how sectional interests threatened the unity of the new republic. The willingness of eastern states to gain economic privileges for themselves and to give up commercial traffic on the Mississippi angered western settlers. Many wondered why they should be loyal to the United States.

JOHN JAY *was a New York politician who favored eastern commerce over western expansion.*

THIS SHIP IS BEING LAUNCHED *from Salem, Massachusetts, one of the major ports of the Northeast.*

Secret Agent Number 13

Conspiracies to separate from the Union were widespread in the West. The most malevolent plotter was James Wilkinson, one of Thomas Jefferson's friends.

After serving as a brigadier general in the Revolutionary War, Wilkinson had emigrated with his family from Maryland to Kentucky. He hoped to make a fortune by sending and selling boatloads of slaves and flour, butter, bacon, and tobacco down the Mississippi River. However, his business ventures were not successful. In 1787 he met with Spanish officials in New Orleans, swore loyalty to the King of Spain, and was placed on the Spanish payroll as their secret Agent Number 13, with a concealed salary of $2,000 a year. Worried that his perfidy would be discovered, Agent Number 13 developed a code: a jumble of numbers and letters that he used when writing to Spanish officials.

JAMES WILKINSON *of Maryland was Spain's secret Agent Number 13.*

His advice to them was worth deciphering and translating from English to Spanish. For example, in 1790 when the United States government planned to build an overland route from Kentucky to New Orleans, Spanish Governor Esteban Miró took Wilkinson's advice: He directed Creek Indians to attack an American scouting party. As a result, there were killings, and plans for the road were abandoned. This was just one of the ways Wilkinson was useful to Spain.[3]

Although he wanted to stop United States government plans for expansion, Wilkinson advised Spanish officials to

36

encourage people from the United States to settle in Louisiana. New citizens of Louisiana were offered free land and the right to sell their products in royal warehouses. Circulars distributed in the United States described the advantages Americans would enjoy by moving to Louisiana and becoming Spanish citizens.

During this time, Thomas Jefferson was George Washington's Secretary of State (1790 to 1793). Jefferson felt confident that the territory of Louisiana would eventually fall from the "feeble" hands of Spain and be acquired "piece by piece" by Americans.[4] His main fear was that the British might swoop down from Canada and take the territory before Americans had a chance to claim it.

Instead of being dismayed by the exodus of Americans who were settling on Spanish-held land, Jefferson was enthusiastic. "I wish a hundred thousand of our inhabitants would accept the invitation [from the Spanish]," he wrote. "It will be the means of delivery to us peaceably, what may otherwise cost us a war."[5] He was pleased at the possibility of taking over Louisiana not by military conquest but by flooding it with American colonists.

Indeed, a steady steam of Americans did come to Louisiana, and they stayed—as loyal American citizens.

THE BATEAU *was a familiar sight on the Mississippi River.*

4 A French Conspiracy

THE SPANISH GOVERNMENT IN LOUISIANA felt threatened not only by American settlers but also by a succession of new rulers in France who held power during the French Revolution (1789 to 1799). Even before Napoleon became the country's dictator, French leaders deplored the loss of Louisiana to Spain and wanted to regain possession of that land.

In 1793 the new French Republic dispatched Citizen Edmond Charles Édouard Genêt as Minister to the United States. (Citizen was a form of address used by revolutionary France to indicate the equality of all men.) Genêt's instructions were to "germinate the principles of liberty and independence in Louisiana"—by conquering it![1] Genêt was also instructed to use the United States as a base of operations against both England and Spain.

Although he represented a country that had revolted against the excesses of an extravagant monarchy, when he landed in Charleston, South Carolina, on April 8, 1793, Genêt looked more like a courtier from the palace of Versailles than a member of a new democracy. Gorgeously attired with gold epaulets, a satin waistcoat, and a flowered cravat (though not wearing his diamond knee buckles), this glamorous visitor was welcomed with wild enthusiasm by crowds sympathetic to France.

CITIZEN GENÊT, *a Frenchman who plotted to regain Louisiana for France, is honored at a party.*

Within a few days of his arrival, Genêt commissioned four privately owned ships—one of them christened *Citizen Genêt*—to capture English and Spanish ships and man them with pro-French Americans. He also dispatched people to organize an army. The French government had given Genêt 250 blank military commissions to use for enlisting Americans whom he would lead in liberating Louisiana from Spain—for France!

Defying President Washington

In 1793, to keep the United States out of war, President Washington issued a proclamation of neutrality that forbade Americans from aiding France, England, and other foreign belligerents. When Genêt sent Americans into Louisiana expecting them to stir up trouble in Spanish-held land, he was violating the President's policy.

Upon learning about Genêt's intrigues, President Washington was furious. He issued a protest to Genêt. The French minister was not flustered. Instead, he became indignant and sent angry letters to Philadelphia and New York newspapers defending his actions. Defying America's Commander in Chief did not faze him because he mistakenly believed that people were on his side. He did not realize that the man he called "Old Washington" was loved and revered as the nation's leader.

A Collaborator

Genêt enlisted the aid of André Michaux, a French botanist who had been in the United States since 1785 studying American trees, shrubs, and plants. In 1793 Michaux expected to embark on a scientific expedition that would take him west of the Mississippi River. Michaux carried two letters from Secretary of State Thomas Jefferson. One requested Governor Isaac Shelby of Kentucky to welcome the eminent botanist. The other letter instructed Michaux to study plants and describe animals that

PRESIDENT GEORGE WASHINGTON *was idolized by the American people but belittled by Genêt.*

might include llamas and mammoths six times the size of elephants. Jefferson speculated that beasts of this kind might inhabit the western wilderness.

Michaux was sponsored by the American Philosophical Society of Philadelphia. Thomas Jefferson, its vice president, collected money for Michaux's expenses from President Washington, Alexander Hamilton, and other members of this learned organization. According to Jefferson's instructions, the botanist's chief goal was to find "the shortest and most convenient route between the United States and the Pacific Ocean."[2]

Michaux was cautioned not to cause trouble while traveling on Spanish soil.

Jefferson did not know that Michaux had been authorized by Genêt to hand out French military commissions to Americans.

During his years in France as minister for the United States (1785 to 1789), Jefferson had been charmed by the French people. He had witnessed the early stages of the French Revolution with approval, commending its goals of "liberty, equality, fraternity." His initial reactions to both Genêt and Michaux were favorable.

Jefferson was disillusioned when Spanish officials learned of Michaux's intentions and sent a protest to the American government. He realized that Michaux and Genêt were in collusion, working to help plan an invasion of Spanish Louisiana.

In July 1793 a French ship towed a captured British vessel into Philadelphia. Genêt planned to arm it to attack Louisiana. When Jefferson protested, Genêt ignored him.

Jefferson and Washington were in a fury. Washington asked that France recall Minister Genêt. At the same time, the French government, disgusted with Genêt, dismissed him because he had angered President Washington and exposed France to the possibility of an unwanted war against the United States. And so this French plot was quashed.[3]

THOMAS JEFFERSON, *who favored relations with France, at first welcomed Genêt.*

5 Avoiding War

THE NEW UNITED STATES HAD DIFFICULT PROBLEMS with the three largest nations of western Europe: England, France, and Spain. Two distinct political parties emerged because Americans vehemently disagreed about foreign policy:

Federalists, led by Alexander Hamilton, supported England as the defender of social order and the source of profitable commerce. They opposed France and were appalled by its bloody revolution. Federalist Party members were merchants, shipowners, and prosperous city dwellers in the East.

Republicans, headed by Thomas Jefferson, were fervently pro-French, favored trade with France, and condemned dealing with their former enemy England. Republican Party members were landowners, farmers, and pioneers.[1]

Treaties with England and Spain

Washington's proclamation of neutrality, which had been ignored by Genêt, was also disregarded by the British. They kept seizing American ships and forcing U.S. sailors to serve in the British Navy. England also persisted in maintaining trading posts and forts along the southern side of the Great Lakes— land that was within the boundaries of the United States.

ALEXANDER HAMILTON *led the Federalist Party, which supported England and opposed the pro-French Republican Party.*
Left: British and French disregard for American neutrality led to battles at sea.

CAPTIVE AMERICAN SAILORS
*were impressed, or forced to serve,
in the British Navy.*

President Washington sent John Jay to London in 1794 to resolve these problems and preserve peace with England. After negotiating for a year, Jay returned to the United States with a treaty that guaranteed good relations with the British. Article I stated, "There shall be a firm, inviolable and universal peace, and a true and sincere friendship between His Britannic Majesty . . . and the United States of America."[2] Subsequent clauses of the Jay Treaty specified that British posts and forts on United States territory would be evacuated. Also, land that stretched north from Ohio to Canada and west from the Appalachians to the Mississippi River was officially—and belatedly—acknowledged by England to be part of the United States. Even though Jay's negotiations didn't solve problems that involved stopping ships and forcing sailors into service, American neutrality was preserved, and trade with England received a big boost.

The Jay Treaty of 1795 was applauded by pro-British Federalists. They were pleased by Jay's negotiations, but pro-French Republicans denounced Jay as a villain whose biased diplomacy could ruin the nation. They cursed him as a man who had betrayed his country by surrendering to England, and they demonstrated their hatred throughout the country by hanging and burning effigies, stuffed figures that looked like Jay.

The Jay Treaty also upset Spanish officials, who worried that the British might work with the United States to seize Louisiana and then divide the spoils. Spain wanted to establish a "firm and inviolable Peace and sincere Friendship" with the United States to counterbalance British influence.[3] And so it agreed to the Pinckney Treaty of 1795, which guaranteed Americans the right to navigate the Lower Mississippi and made New Orleans a duty-free port. Spain accepted the 31st parallel as the southern boundary of the United States. This stretched American borders as far south as Natchez, Tennessee, and eased the path for

ANGRY MOBS *made effigies of John Jay, which they hanged and burned.*

pioneers seeking new lands (now part of Mississippi and Alabama). Westerners and members of the Republican Party cheered the Pinckney Treaty.

The Undeclared War with France

Both of these treaties were very disturbing to France because they enhanced the powers of England and Spain in North America. However, France needed soldiers to put down riots in Paris and to fight a war in Austria. Troops could not be spared to invade the United States.

Instead, officials in France decided to seize American ships under the pretext that the United States was trading with its enemy England. French leaders made matters worse in 1797 when they declared that any Americans found serving under an enemy flag would be treated as pirates, and that all American vessels would be "lawful prizes" if they didn't carry complete lists of crew and passengers.

French cruisers captured hundreds of American ships.

France was engaged in a state of undeclared naval war against the United States, called the quasi war.

When John Adams became President in 1797, he hoped he could end French raids on American commerce without fighting a full-scale war. Deciding to use diplomacy, he sent three envoys to France: Charles Pinckney from South Carolina, Elbridge Gerry from Massachusetts, and John Marshall from Virginia.

The American mission was badly timed. When the men arrived in Paris in October 1797, France's government, which was constantly changing, was being ruled by a five-man Directory. All attention was focused on General Napoleon Bonaparte, idol and hero of France. This 28-year-old military genius had been victorious in Italy and was successfully fighting in Austria.

THREE AMERICAN ENVOYS *to France (from left to right): Charles Pinckney, Elbridge Gerry, and John Marshall, tried to negotiate an end to the quasi war.*

Talleyrand was the Directory's Minister of Foreign Affairs. After returning from two years of exile in the United States, he'd used his charm, cleverness, and social contacts to get back into the center of France's political arena. The Directory believed that this cunning aristocrat was ideally qualified to deal with the envoys because he had lived in America.

Having traveled from Maine to Virginia, Talleyrand boasted about his first-hand knowledge of the new nation. He was so contemptuous of Americans that he declared that "refinement does not exist" in the United States.[4] He described its inhabitants as grossly materialistic, uncultured, and uncouth.

Talleyrand dreaded the prospect of people like that populating more territory. To keep them from spilling across their borders, he believed that France should control all of Louisiana.

The XYZ Affair

Talleyrand kept the three American envoys waiting for two weeks before there was any sign of negotiations to end the quasi war. At different times, three of Talleyrand's agents told the

Americans that peace could be obtained by paying a bribe.

Talleyrand's go-betweens kept insisting that hostilities against Americans would end after the bribe was paid. Pressed for a response, an exasperated Pinckney reportedly blurted out, "It is no, no; not a sixpence."[5]

When the American envoys returned to the United States in 1798, they delivered a detailed report to President Adams. The letters X, Y, and Z were substituted for the names of the three agents who had asked for bribes.

An angry President Adams denounced France, declaring that "hostilities should be avowed in a formal Declaration of War."[6]

Twelve hundred men marched to the President's home in Philadelphia to volunteer their services.[7] Hundreds in Boston clamored to defend their country. The mood was so anti-French

THE DIRECTORY *met in the ornate Palace of Luxembourg, in Paris.*

TALLEYRAND WAS SO CUNNING *that he had power in France before and after the French Revolution.*

that audiences refused to listen to French music, and French exiles feared for their own safety. Clusters of black ribbons, adopted as anti-French badges, were seen on women's hats and men's lapels.

Jefferson called the anti-French frenzy an "X. Y. Z. fever," but it became known as the XYZ Affair.

As a result of the XYZ Affair, Congress created the Department of the Navy. It also authorized the President to create an army of 50,000 soldiers, should war be declared. Alexander Hamilton campaigned to be second-in-command of a provisional army under General Washington. He had proved his worth as an Army officer during the Revolutionary War and was anxious to return to the battlefield fighting France.

By the summer of 1798, Americans waited for aggressive actions from France that would compel them to declare war.

When news about the XYZ Affair reached Paris, there was quite a commotion. To protect himself, Talleyrand insisted that the American envoys had been duped by impostors and called accusations against him "ridiculous."

The Directory asked President Adams to send new envoys to negotiate a peaceful agreement. By the time the American mission reached Paris in 1800, General Napoleon Bonaparte had seized power. On November 9, 1799, Napoleon had used force to overthrow the Directory. He replaced it with a new government called the Consulate, consisting of three consuls: Napoleon— and two others who were mere figureheads.

First Consul Napoleon ruled with a tyrannical authority that surpassed the power of any king. World conquest was his goal: Europe first, then the other continents. Napoleon believed that peace with the United States was crucial to his plans.[8]

Still, negotiations had to be delayed because Napoleon was leading his armies across the Alps in new campaigns against the Austrians. Finally, when this military hero returned to Paris, a treaty with the United States was approved and signed by him, and the quasi war ended. This took place on September 30, 1800.

That very next day a secret treaty was signed that transferred Louisiana from Spain to France.

NAPOLEON WANTED TO CONQUER *the world. In this cartoon John Bull, who represents England, is trying to stop him.*

Oh who is it dares interupt me in my Progreſs

why 'tis I little Johnny Bull Protecting a little spot I clap my hand on and d — n. me if you come any farther that's all

THREE AMERICANS *(left) try to negotiate with a five-headed monster that represents the Directory, which ruled France in 1797.*

6 A Tyrant's Treaty

AT THE SAME TIME THAT HIS AGENTS WERE NEGOTIATING with the
United States to end the quasi war, Napoleon had other agents
in Madrid who were instructed to acquire the enormous area of
Louisiana for France. Talks with the Spanish royal family began
during the summer of 1800.

The King, Charles IV, had little interest in political matters.
He was said to be so ignorant that he did not even know that
an American Revolution had taken place. When not engaged in
daily six-hour hunts that involved the company of approximately
one thousand aides, he spent his time repairing watches, working as a carpenter, forging armor, enjoying card games, playing
the violin (very badly), eating enormous meals, praying,
and napping.

The Queen, Maria Luisa, was different. She was driven by
aspirations, not just for Spain, but for her family. The Queen
dominated political decision-making. Aided by advisers, Her
Royal Highness negotiated with Napoleon's Minister to Spain.
King Charles sat in on some conferences to echo his wife's
statements and make negotiations official.

SPAIN'S KING CHARLES IV *and
Queen Maria Luisa are shown
with two of their children.*

Much to the Queen's delight, Napoleon offered her land in
Tuscany. To be called the Kingdom of Etruria, it would be ruled

by her darling daughter Luisetta and her son-in-law, Luis. The acquisition of Italian territory for the family was deliciously satisfying, not only because a throne was set up for her child, but also because the Spanish Queen had a special affection for northern Italy. She had been born and brought up there. It was with great pride and pleasure that Her Royal Highness anticipated having her precious daughter become queen of a realm that was said to have more than one million subjects.

In return for this Italian land, Napoleon was to receive all of Spanish Louisiana.

The King and Queen of Spain were overjoyed. They were sure they had hoodwinked the great Napoleon by swapping miserable Mississippi swampland for glorious Etruria. Therefore, when the Treaty of San Ildefonso was negotiated in 1800, the Spanish government not only gladly got rid of its vast North American territory, but, to equalize the deal, it agreed to give France six huge warships.

France had swapped a small section of Italy for Louisiana and half a dozen ships! Spanish officials had no control over their Queen's decisions, and Napoleon was too mighty to be challenged. Perhaps having Napoleon as an ally occupying this land would prove to be an asset. Governing and policing Louisiana had been draining the Spanish treasury. Now Napoleon would take over the expense of protecting the area that separated the United States from Spain's silver-rich holdings in Mexico. Napoleon, the most powerful man in the world, could prevent both the Americans and the British from gaining ground in the Western Hemisphere.

In a verbal agreement made at the time of the Treaty of San Ildefonso, Napoleon solemnly promised that he would not sell or give away the land of Louisiana to any other nation—unless he wished to return it to Spain. He also agreed that the treaty would become valid only after other European countries recognized Etruria as a new nation.

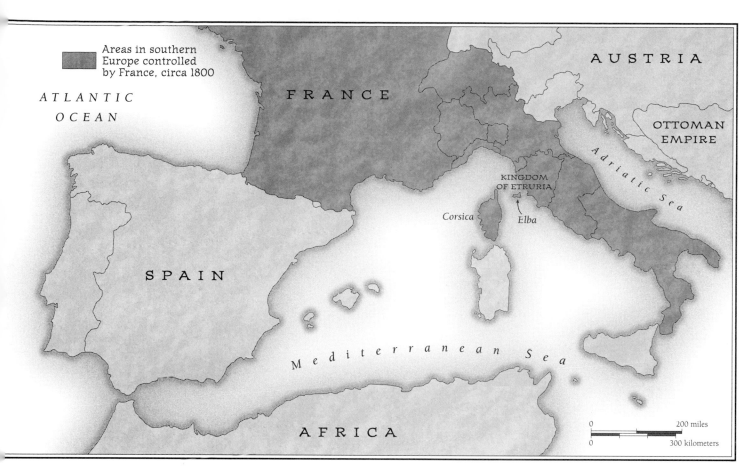

Areas in southern
Europe controlled
by France, circa 1800

ATLANTIC
OCEAN

FRANCE

AUSTRIA

OTTOMAN
EMPIRE

Adriatic Sea

KINGDOM
OF ETRURIA

Corsica   Elba

SPAIN

Mediterranean   Sea

AFRICA

0   200 miles

0   300 kilometers

NAPOLEON PROMISED *the
Kingdom of Etruria to Spain
in exchange for Louisiana.*

Napoleon insisted that secrecy regarding the Treaty of San
Ildefonso was crucial. If the Americans found out, they might
attack the feeble forces of Spanish Louisiana rather than wait
until Napoleon's aggressive, disciplined troops were at their
frontier. And it could lead to catastrophe if the British learned
about it: England's Navy might attack New Orleans, and enemy
troops might occupy the entire Mississippi Valley.

Bonaparte was in no hurry to occupy his new North American
possession until he made peace with England, a country the
French had been fighting since 1793.

The Spanish monarchs were so cowed by Napoleon that
they delivered Louisiana to him before he handed over Etruria.

When their son-in-law and daughter arrived in Tuscany to
become King and Queen of Etruria, French armies occupied
the land, French generals governed it, and no foreign power
recognized this new kingdom.

The new Queen found the palace in shambles, stripped of its furnishings.

Sympathetic noblemen supplied chandeliers, draperies, furniture, chinaware, and other household equipment.

Luisetta was humiliated. She disclosed that "this was the first time that the daughter of the King of Spain, accustomed to being served in gold and silver, saw herself obliged to eat off porcelain."[1] One month after Luisetta's arrival, French officials forced her to discharge her Spanish retinue. She "could not succeed in retaining . . . a single Spanish lady."[2]

Napoleon officially owned Louisiana, and he controlled Etruria, too.[3] He had stacked his cards against royalty and placed a king and queen at the bottom of the deck.

Luisetta's husband died one year after ascending the throne. At the age of 22, a royal daughter of Spain was supposed to be the sole ruler of Etruria. However, "Napoleon was determined to keep the whole of Italy [including Etruria] under his dominion."[4] French officials ruled, guided by "the power of so atrocious a tyrant [Napoleon]." Summing up her sorrow, Luisetta wrote, "I have been the unhappy victim of the blackest treachery, the puppet of a tyrant, who made sport of our lives and our properties."[5]

Bonaparte's next move was establishing a powerful French empire in the Western Hemisphere.

IN THIS CARTOON, *Napoleon clearly outweighs British power.*

⁊ The "Black Napoleon"

TOUSSAINT L'OUVERTURE was idolized by his followers, who called him the "Black Napoleon." In the portrait of Toussaint on horseback, the shackles on the ground remind us that he was once a slave.

BEFORE OCCUPYING LOUISIANA, Napoleon planned to gain complete control over St. Domingue (present-day Haiti). As France's most valuable colony in the Caribbean, it would be a rest stop and supply center for ships headed for the North American continent.[1]

It galled Bonaparte that although St. Domingue was owned by France, it was being ruled by a former slave, General Toussaint L'Ouverture, who was hailed by his followers as the "Black Napoleon."

Before slave rebellions erupted in 1791, forty thousand French people and several thousand "free persons of color" occupying St. Domingue owned half a million slaves. About half of the "free persons of color" were mulattoes (racially mixed). The other half were former slaves who had purchased their own freedom or had been given freedom by their masters. Some slaves were domestic servants, but most of them labored on plantations that raised indigo, coffee, cotton, and sugarcane.

Since knowledge can lead to dangerous desires for freedom, slaves were forbidden to learn how to read and write.

Sugar was the main product that sweetened the French economy. It also made the lives of countless blacks bitter beyond belief. A visitor reported one shockingly brutal scene: "There were about a hundred men and women of different ages, all occupied in digging ditches in a cane-field, the majority of them naked or covered with rags. . . . Several foremen armed with long whips moved periodically between them, giving stinging blows to all who, worn out by fatigue, were compelled to take a rest—men or women, young or old."[2]

Field hands endured harsh, hopeless lives. Laboring from dawn to dusk, they were poorly fed, beaten, and sometimes tortured. Mass executions killed thousands of slaves each year. Plantation owners knew they could readily be replaced by constant supplies of human beings who survived agonizing ocean voyages from Africa. Stacked like lumber in the holds of ships, many died of starvation or from diseases caused by filth, foul air, and overcrowding.

SLAVES WORKED LONG HOURS *cutting sugarcane, the chief crop of most Caribbean islands.*

CRUEL TREATMENT *of slaves was common.*

Only the strongest disembarked, to be purchased at auctions by the highest bidders.

Slave uprisings became common and persisted throughout the 17th and 18th centuries. Invariably these revolts were crushed by the power and savagery of plantation owners. In the revolt of 1791, however, hundreds of whites were killed, and their plantations destroyed. Blacks controlled almost all of St. Domingue.

The major leader to emerge from this revolution was Toussaint L'Ouverture, a 47-year-old former slave. This remarkable person had been owned by a humane man and worked as a livestock handler and coachman. A priest who was impressed by this slave's extraordinary intelligence broke the law by teaching him to read and write.

PRESIDENT JOHN ADAMS
sympathized with Toussaint.

During the 1791 slave uprising, Toussaint used his knowledge of herbal healing to act as chief medical officer. In 1793 he recruited an army of his own and was hailed as its general. In command of rebels consisting of slaves and maroons (escaped slaves who hid in the wilderness), he became famous for his guerrilla warfare surprise attacks against superior enemy forces.

Toussaint adopted the name L'Ouverture ("The Opening") because he opened the way to freedom for his people.

In 1794, fearing the loss of its richest colony, the government in Paris declared that slavery was abolished in St. Domingue. As a result, Toussaint gave his allegiance to France and was appointed a general in the French Republican Army.

Acting like a leader of an independent country, Toussaint sent an envoy to the United States to ask President John Adams for military and economic aid. The President wanted "some kind of agreement" with the rebellious black leader, because an alliance with Toussaint could become both strategically useful and a source of profitable trade.[3]

In 1799 Adams signed a treaty with Toussaint to establish trade. In return for munitions and provisions from the United States, the "Black Napoleon" agreed to keep slave revolts from spreading to the southern United States.[4]

By 1801 Toussaint had become dictator of the entire island.[5] Although his official title was Governor-General, he acted like a king. Copying the pomp and ceremony of monarchs, he built a palace for himself, dressed in the finery of a European aristocrat, and surrounded himself with bodyguards who were clothed in colorful, full-dress French uniforms.

Rather than risk proclaiming complete independence, Toussaint declared he was a loyal French citizen and asserted that the island was a protectorate of the French Republic that he was protecting.

However, he stored ammunition just in case Napoleon decided to send troops.

Ex-slaves Defeat Napoleon's Troops

Napoleon detested Toussaint. It was galling for him to learn that this black dictator had proclaimed laws without his approval. Toussaint was leading the island to independence. Bonaparte was convinced that if France recognized this ex-slave as a ruler "the scepter of the new world would sooner or later . . . [fall] into the hands of the blacks."[6]

France needed complete control over the wealth of St. Domingue. Therefore, Toussaint would have to be ousted.

Bonaparte's resolve to control St. Domingue was cheered on by his wife, Josephine.

She had been born on the Caribbean island of Martinique, and her family owned a plantation in St. Domingue. Josephine wrote letters to Toussaint asking him to guard her family's property and to send her the profits.

Napoleon did not object to his wife's relationship with the black dictator. He, too, feigned friendship—but to catch his enemy off guard. While planning an invasion and the return of slavery to St. Domingue, he wrote to Toussaint: "We have conceived esteem for you, and we take pleasure in recognizing and proclaiming the great services you have rendered to the French people. . . . What do you desire? The liberty of the blacks? You know that in all the countries we have been, we have given it to the people who do as we wish."[7]

Napoleon placed his brother-in-law General Charles Victor Emmanuel Leclerc in command of a campaign against Toussaint. Leclerc headed the largest expeditionary force that France

GENERAL LECLERC *was Napoleon's brother-in-law.*

WHAT'S THE DEAL?

had ever sent overseas. He was in charge of almost 30,000 men who were to take over St. Domingue, do away with Toussaint, and restore slavery. After conquering this Caribbean colony, Leclerc was to set his sights on Louisiana and play a heroic role in establishing a glorious French empire in North America.

Leclerc's expedition was prepared with the greatest secrecy. Setting sail in high spirits, he anticipated easy victory. His wife, Napoleon's beautiful sister Pauline, accompanied him on the warship as though she were on a pleasure cruise. She brought along their four-year-old son and a staff of their household help. Anticipating the Caribbean venture with delight, she engaged actors, dancers, and musicians to join the voyagers. Gorgeous gowns, crates of china, crystal, linens, bales of silks, and sets of furniture were carried in the ship's hold alongside munitions.

As soon as her husband got rid of Toussaint and established order, Pauline intended to move into a palace, live in luxury, and enliven society with lavish parties.

Leclerc's ships reached Cap Haitien and Port-au-Prince in February 1802. Both of these St. Domingue ports had been set on fire and inhabitants had been massacred by a black commander, Henri Christophe (later King of Haiti). When the French disembarked, they marched over smoking ruins past piles of mutilated white corpses. Toussaint and his generals had decided to kill their enemies and burn plantations and towns to stop the invaders by depriving them of food and shelter.

Leclerc was appalled. His wife, Pauline, was aghast. Instead of living in a paradise where she could dazzle others with her charms and entertain them with extreme extravagance, she had to move into an old stone structure that looked like a fortress.

Toussaint's followers were determined. They destroyed roads and threw corpses into wells to contaminate the water. They burned everything, even their own homes, so that nothing would be left to feed and shelter the invaders. Led by Toussaint, both men and women fought ferociously against crack French

JOSEPHINE, Napoleon's wife, entertained Toussaint's sons while they were in Paris attending school.

HOMES AND PROPERTY in
*St. Domingue were burned during
the French invasion.*

ALL OF ST. DOMINGUE
was involved in the fighting.

troops and used ambushes to kill them. Snipers seemed to lurk behind every rock and tree. Old people who approached the French soldiers supposedly to sell fruit, suddenly stabbed and shot them. Children, seemingly at play, attacked to kill when an enemy walked by.

The French lost thousands of men both from battle and from yellow fever. (Most natives were immune to this disease.) Toussaint was winning.

In June 1802, the French invited Toussaint to a "conference." As soon as he entered French headquarters, he was surrounded by soldiers, tied up, dragged to the waterfront, and forced to board a ship bound for France.

Toussaint was sent by coach to Fort de Joux, a medieval structure high in the French Alps. He was locked up in a cold, damp, windowless cell. As a result of being starved and abused by his jailkeeper, he died there in April 1803.

Toussaint's arrest incited his people to fight on.

In September 1802, Leclerc wrote to Napoleon that of 28,300 men, only 4,000 were fit for service; that "the occupation of St. Domingue has cost us till now twenty-four thousand men."[8] One month later he again expressed his desperation by requesting 12,000 additional soldiers. He advised Napoleon, ". . . If you cannot send the troops I demand . . . [the colony] will be forever lost to France."[9]

Leclerc died of yellow fever on November 2, 1802. Napoleon did not learn of his death and the destruction of his troops until January 7, 1803. Bonaparte dispatched General Rochambeau to replace Leclerc and sent reinforcements of 20,000 additional soldiers.

By November 1803, due to casualties from battle and from

yellow fever, Rochambeau surrendered. France was forced to leave the island.

St. Domingue, the future Haiti, became an independent nation ruled by blacks.

Napoleon's troops had been defeated by former slaves who had never been trained to be a unified army. Black guerrilla fighters had prevented France's well-disciplined soldiers from proceeding to occupy land that was adjacent to the United States.

NAPOLEON WAS DETERMINED *to be the most powerful man in the world.*

73

8 Jefferson's Minister to France

IN 1801, THE FIRST YEAR OF HIS PRESIDENCY, Thomas Jefferson was alarmed at unconfirmed reports that France had obtained all of Louisiana from Spain through a secret treaty. He foresaw that should this be true, "it would be impossible that France and the United States can continue long as friends."[1]

Jefferson turned for help to his dear friend Robert Livingston, a statesman who had served in the Continental Congress and had helped him draft the Declaration of Independence. Even though Livingston was quite deaf and couldn't speak French well, Jefferson was confident that his friend's charm, brilliance, and diplomatic tact qualified him to be an outstanding Minister to France.[2]

Livingston set sail from New York harbor on October 15, 1801. His wife, two daughters, their husbands, and servants accompanied him. To move his elegant household, he needed a mountain of luggage. He also brought along "poultry, hogs, sheep, & a cow and a calf" to be used for fresh meat. His carriage, lashed to the quarterdeck, served as a sitting room for the ladies. The one-month sea voyage was unsettling for the women, who were seasick much of the time.[3]

According to his instructions, Livingston was expected to discourage the French government from acquiring Louisiana,

AS PRESIDENT, THOMAS JEFFERSON *(above) appointed Robert Livingston (right) to be his Minister to France.*

because it would jeopardize its friendly relationship with the United States.

This message had to be relayed to the great Napoleon.

Shortly after his arrival in Paris, Livingston had a meeting with Talleyrand. This corrupt, conniving, charismatic character was now Napoleon's Minister of Foreign Affairs. During his talk with Livingston, Talleyrand acted arrogantly. He refused to admit that any treaty between France and Spain had been signed and denied the fact by remarking, "It has been a subject of conversation, but nothing concluded."[4]

Meanwhile, news confirming the existence of the treaty had become widespread.

Livingston was presented to Bonaparte on December 6, 1801, the day after his meeting with Talleyrand. Napoleon greeted him in the ornate audience room of the Tuileries Palace. This was strictly a social occasion. Other diplomats were present, and only a brief conversation took place.

Upon learning that Livingston had never been to Europe before, Napoleon is reported to have said, "You have come to a very corrupt world," and then with dark humor, knowing of Talleyrand's reputation for bribe-taking, he quipped that Talleyrand was qualified to explain the meaning of the word "corruption."[5]

Livingston realized that discussions about Louisiana had to be conveyed through people who could influence Napoleon. Talleyrand would not be helpful. Therefore, Livingston deliberately developed a close relationship with Napoleon's older brother, Joseph, who exercised some authority in affairs of state. However, when the subject of Louisiana was broached, Joseph remarked that his influence was very limited, that Napoleon was "his own counselor."[6]

JOSEPH BONAPARTE
was Napoleon's older brother.

Months dragged on with no reaction from Napoleon.

Frustrated, Livingston wrote to Secretary of State James Madison, "There never was a government in which less could be done by negotiation than here. There is no people, no legislature, no counsellors. One man [Napoleon] is everything. He seldom asks advice, and never hears it unasked. His ministers are mere clerks; and his legislature and counsellors parade officers."[7]

Talleyrand kept denying that France owned Louisiana.

Ignoring him, in March 1802—one month after Leclerc reached St. Domingue—Livingston wrote to Madison to say that French authorities intended to occupy Louisiana and planned "to have a leading interest in the politics of our western country."[8]

In April he wrote that 5,000 or 7,000 French troops were expected to land in New Orleans after stopping at St. Domingue.

JAMES MADISON, *Jefferson's Secretary of State, hoped Livingston would be able to buy New Orleans from the French.*

"This Affair of Louisiana"

President Jefferson was distressed to learn that Napoleon's troops would occupy land adjacent to the United States. He was agitated by the prospect of France controlling New Orleans. Thousands of American Westerners needed this port for their economic survival. It was urgent that his Minister to France understand that there was a national crisis. The following statements were in a letter he wrote to Robert Livingston in April 1802:

"There is on the globe one spot the possessor of which is our natural and habitual enemy. It is New Orleans, through which the produce of three-eighths of our territory must pass to market.

"The day that France takes possession of New Orleans fixes the sentence. . . . From that moment, we must marry ourselves to the British fleet and nation.

"Every eye in the U.S. is now fixed on this affair of Louisiana. Perhaps nothing since the Revolutionary War has produced more uneasy sensations through the body of the nation."[9]

Jefferson also wrote that trouble could be avoided if France gave New Orleans and the Floridas to the United States. (He did not know that Spain had refused to give the Floridas to Napoleon.)

This letter might have been intended for the eyes of French intelligence agents. It is possible that Jefferson wanted Livingston to pass it on to them so that they could read its threatening contents and report that the United States was a belligerent nation ready to be allied with England against France. The letter might have been written as a ruse because Jefferson definitely did not want war.

In May, confirmation that the French had obtained Louisiana from Spain came by way of Rufus King, the U.S. Minister to England, who had sent a copy of the Treaty of San Ildefonso to officials in Washington.

Secretary of State Madison sent a letter to Livingston expressing concern that a French Louisiana would be disastrous. He wanted Livingston to ask the price of New Orleans and of the Floridas. (He, too, mistakenly believed the Floridas belonged to France.) However, Madison omitted an important directive: He did not give Livingston authority to purchase foreign-owned property, possibly because acquiring it was considered to be unconstitutional.

In June, Napoleon ordered his Minister of the Navy, Admiral Denis Decrès, to organize a military invasion. "My intention," he declared, ". . .[is] that we take possession of Louisiana with the least possible delay, and that it have the appearance of being directed to Santo Domingo [St. Domingue]."[10]

General Claude Victor was chosen as commander and named chief military officer of Louisiana. French troops were readied to set out for New Orleans from a port in Holland. Ships were scheduled to sail in September 1802.

General Victor was dismayed when he found that many of these ships had already left to take soldiers and supplies to St. Domingue. He couldn't sail as planned.

Napoleon was in a huff about the delay. From his viewpoint, there was no excuse for postponing an important mission.

Through newspaper articles, Americans learned that France might be their new neighbor. Having weak Spain in the country's backyard was no threat. But Napoleon's troops!

Many readers panicked. Some clamored for war. Others warned that if the United States failed to take and claim New Orleans, they would separate from the Union. They'd form an independent nation—or shift their allegiance to whatever country controlled New Orleans.

Livingston prepared a long pamphlet called "Whether It Will Be Advantageous to France to Take Possession of Louisiana."

He warned Napoleon's advisers: Should France occupy Louisiana, the United States would become England's ally. This could result in war against the French.

Livingston offered a peaceful solution: If the French insisted on occupying Louisiana, they could cede New Orleans to the United States. Americans would promise to make the port duty-free for both France's ships and its products. As a result, the French would have all the advantages of an important New World port without paying to maintain it.[11]

Napoleon was not swayed by Livingston's arguments. He had not yet received news that his troops in St. Domingue were being slaughtered. The great Bonaparte still intended to use the colony as a stepping-stone to New Orleans.

9 A National Crisis

SPANISH ADMINISTRATOR *Juan Ventura Morales infuriated Americans by closing the port of New Orleans to U.S. shipping. Right: Americans prepare for a war to defend commerce.*

ON OCTOBER 15, 1802, Spain's King Charles IV was so intimidated by Napoleon's power that he signed a royal decree that *officially* transferred Louisiana to France.[1] The next day in New Orleans, Spanish administrator Juan Ventura Morales acted on a very secret royal order and closed the port to United States shipping by taking away the right of deposit: the right to store cargo in New Orleans warehouses. This meant that American merchandise would not be safely locked up and that farm products would rot in port before being transferred from river flatboats to seagoing ships anchored and waiting in the harbor.

Morales was upset because Americans were smuggling Spanish gold and silver coins out of New Orleans into the United States. He was also annoyed that Americans had been using the port free of charge. He wrote reporting these facts to King Charles, who signed the decree stopping the right of deposit in July. The decree took three months—until October—to reach New Orleans.

Taking away the right of deposit caused an uproar in the United States. It released tirades of condemnation from congressmen and newspaper editors.

Many critics blamed Napoleon. They were positive that Morales was obeying the wishes of the French tyrant and

A POLITICAL CARTOON shows
Federalist and Republican congressmen
fighting over issues of the time.

furious that France could have such control of their destinies.

Westerners warned Congress, "No power in the world should deprive us of our rights. . . . If our liberty in this matter is disputed, nothing shall prevent our taking possession of New Orleans."[2]

Southerners were also in an uproar. A reporter for the *Charleston Courier* wrote that Americans would be justified "in taking possession of the port in question . . . by force of arms."[3]

Easterners, too, were provoked, because the closure struck a blow at shippers in Atlantic coastal cities who had established trade with New Orleans. Inflammatory articles and pamphlets appeared in eastern coastal states and, not surprisingly, in the

THIS CARTOON *satirizes President Jefferson's effort to avoid war, in spite of the abusive way France and England were treating the United States.*

western states of Ohio, Kentucky, and Tennessee. The *New York Evening Post* told its readers that it was the right of the United States "to regulate the future destiny of North America," and that the nation had "the right to its rivers."[4]

Senator James Ross of Pennsylvania drafted a resolution demanding that the President raise an army of 50,000 men to seize New Orleans before the French arrived to take over the government of Louisiana. Fifty million dollars was to be appropriated for this attack. Ross, like other members of the Federalist Party, was anti-French and anxious for war.

However, the majority in Congress were members of Jefferson's pro-French Republican Party. Even Kentucky and Tennessee frontiersmen surprised people by choosing peace and backing the administration. Their representatives overruled Ross's resolution and substituted a ruling that empowered the President to keep a militia of 80,000 ready to march at a moment's notice, should warfare prove necessary.

Regarding the situation as the most serious crisis that the nation had faced since the end of the American Revolution, President Jefferson wanted to safeguard American interests through negotiations. "Peace is our passion" was one of his assertions.[5] He had to silence the warmongers and ensure peace.

Envoy Extraordinary

To stop storms of protest, and worried that Federalists might "force us into war," Jefferson sent a note to his close friend James Monroe on January 10, 1803. He asked Monroe to become Envoy Extraordinary to France and join Livingston there.[6]

Westerners liked Monroe because he had repeatedly spoken up in favor of free navigation on the Mississippi and was considered to be "one of their best and able advocates."[7] They were gratified by his appointment. He shared their concerns—because he owned extensive tracts of land in Kentucky.

Monroe was also popular in the East. He was known in Washington as a well-qualified diplomat who had previously served as Congressman, Senator, Governor of Virginia, and Minister to France. He was, above all, a dedicated patriot, who had fought with Washington at Valley Forge.

Jefferson wrote to him that all hopes were fixed upon him and that "the future destinies of this republic" depended upon the outcome of his mission.[8]

Monroe was financially strapped. He had debts to pay, and the appointment would force him to give up his law practice. His government salary would be meager. Still, he felt impelled to accept. To meet his immediate expenses, Monroe sold his china and furniture to James Madison. He asked a neighbor to manage his properties in Virginia and Kentucky so that some of the land could be sold, should the need for money became urgent.

Monroe was given a multilayered set of instructions. First, he must offer the sum of 50 million livres ($9,375,000) to buy New Orleans and the Floridas.[9] If that offer was refused, this Envoy Extraordinary should try to purchase New Orleans alone. If Napoleon rejected this proposal, Monroe was merely to insist upon Americans' rights to navigate the entire length of the Mississippi and to store their export goods in New Orleans.

Napoleon could have refused to sell an inch of land. He could have satisfied the demands of the United States just by opening up the river and providing Americans with storage facilities!

If negotiations with France failed, Monroe was instructed to proceed to England and arrange an alliance so that with British aid the United States could take all of Louisiana from the French. British diplomats had already indicated their willingness to fight against France. Pro-war Federalists favored this British-American partnership. At a farewell dinner in honor of Monroe, one guest had offered this well-received toast: "Peace if peace is honorable, war if war is necessary."[10]

Jefferson had another motive for wanting to purchase

JAMES MONROE *was sent by Jefferson to help Livingston negotiate with Napoleon.*

Meriwether Lewis (top) and William Clark explored part of Louisiana while searching for a route to the Pacific Ocean.

Louisiana. His passion for increasing his nation's size was well known. In a message to Congress on January 18, 1803, he requested money to dispatch an expedition "to provide an extension of territory which the rapid increase of our numbers would call for." Jefferson asked Congress for only $2,500 to finance a "Voyage of Discovery" to the shores of the Pacific. Because of the low budget, his request was approved.[11] Jefferson's brilliant secretary, Meriwether Lewis, was ordered to lead the expedition. Lewis chose his friend William Clark as co-leader.

Meanwhile in Holland, storms and icy water in the North Sea now made General Victor's departure for Louisiana impossible. Victor's fleet was icebound.

In January 1803, Napoleon received news that yellow fever had killed his brother-in-law, General Leclerc. He learned that as a result of fighting and yellow fever, thousands of his soldiers had died in St. Domingue. In February Napoleon, refusing to acknowledge weather as a reason for stalling, ordered "the entire expedition to sail directly to New Orleans" without diverting any soldiers to St. Domingue.[12]

During March 1803, ice in the North Sea ports melted, and the French armada was free to sail.

However, there was another setback to Napoleon's transatlantic plans: the threat of war with the British.

King George III of England warned his Parliament that Napoleon's fleet was off the coast of Holland probably preparing to invade the British Isles. British warships were ordered to blockade General Victor's ships and attack them as soon as they headed out.

To avoid battles at sea where the French forces were weak, Bonaparte canceled General Victor's expedition.

Soon after, Napoleon learned that General Rochambeau's troops were being annihilated in St. Domingue. He was distraught.

His glorious dream of a North American empire had become a nightmare.

JEFFERSON WAS EAGER *to learn what Lewis and Clark would discover about the geography and the plants and animals west of the Mississippi.*

WHAT'S THE DEAL?

10 Napoleon Changes His Mind

SEVERE WINTER WEATHER in Europe, a slave revolt in the Caribbean that cost Napoleon his richest colony, and the threat of war with England had kept French troops from occupying the entire Mississippi Valley and changing the course of America's destiny.

Americans' violent opposition to a French occupation of Louisiana was a factor that bothered Napoleon. He dreaded another defeat in the Western Hemisphere. By withdrawing from North America he could remove the major cause of friction between his country and the United States.

At some time during the spring of 1803, Napoleon decided to get rid of Louisiana by selling it to the United States. His immediate aim was taking Egypt from England, and he needed money to wage war.

Although they played important roles in international politics, two of Napoleon's brothers, Joseph and Lucien, had not been consulted about Louisiana. They were horrified when told that Napoleon might sell it. The idea of giving up on a New World empire appalled them, for they both rode on the coattails of Napoleon's successes.

Joseph had his own unscrupulous secret reason for trying to stop the sale of Louisiana. England's Ambassador to France had offered him a bribe of 100,000 British pounds if he could

THIS CARTOON SHOWS NAPOLEON *slicing up Europe as England tries to carve up the rest of the world.*

convince Napoleon to hold onto Louisiana. The bribe was intended to prevent the United States from becoming a world power and also to foster friendship with France.[1]

Joseph and Lucien rushed to the palace in the early-morning hours of April 7, 1803. They dared to interrupt Napoleon, who was luxuriating in a bathtub, immersed to his neck in perfumed water. It was a relief to see this tyrant relaxed. At first the brothers talked about plays and poetry. They reminisced about their childhood on the island of Corsica and chatted about trivial matters. After a while, both Joseph and Lucien spoke their minds. They berated Napoleon for entertaining the idea of selling Louisiana to the United States.

Furious, Napoleon stood up, then threw himself back in the bath with such force that splashes drenched Joseph. Napoleon screamed that he could make decisions without the consent of anyone. Joseph shouted back that he himself would head a movement to block the sale of France's New World colony.

The heated argument was so upsetting to see that a bathroom servant fainted. Attendants were summoned to remove the servant, assist Napoleon out of the bathtub, and dress him. Joseph and Lucien left after seeing that Napoleon was so riled he smashed his own snuffbox by hurling it on the floor.

Several days later, on Easter Sunday, April 10, 1803, Bonaparte summoned Minister of the Navy Denis Decrès and Minister of Finance François de Barbé-Marbois to a conference. These two advisers were well acquainted with America. Decrès had fought in Virginia with the French forces during the

LUCIEN BONAPARTE (below) interrupted Napoleon's bath to tell his brother he was against selling Louisiana.

AN ARTIST'S FANCIFUL VERSION
*of the great Napoleon
taking a bath*

NAPOLEON STANDS LISTENING *while two of his advisers discuss his plan to sell Louisiana to the United States.*

American Revolution. Barbé-Marbois, who had spent many years in Philadelphia as a representative of the French government, was a well-admired friend of George Washington, Alexander Hamilton, James Madison, Thomas Jefferson, Robert Livingston, and James Monroe.

Napoleon wished to hear their comments about the future of Louisiana.

He told them, "I think of ceding it to the United States. . . . I already consider the Colony as completely lost, and it seems to me that in the hands of that growing power [the United States] it will be more useful to the policy, and even to the commerce of France than if I should try to keep it."[2]

He noted that the British had successfully taken Canada from France and controlled rich territories in Asia. They might decide to seize Louisiana, a conquest that would be easy for them because of their tremendous navy and their troops in Canada.

Napoleon predicted that by selling the land to the United States, he would eventually make Americans more powerful than France's hated rival, England.

Minister of the Navy Decrès disagreed with Bonaparte. He argued that there was no port in the world more valuable than New Orleans, and that France should never give up its colony of Louisiana.

Minister of Finance Barbé-Marbois backed Napoleon's views. He declared that the French should get out before they were thrown out of North America by the British or by the Americans. The conference continued through much of the night, and it ended with nothing resolved.

At daybreak Napoleon summoned Barbé-Marbois to his room to announce his decision: "I renounce Louisiana. It is not only New Orleans that I will cede. It is the whole colony without any reservation. I renounce it with the greatest regret."[3]

Bonaparte then directed Barbé-Marbois to negotiate with Livingston.

That very day, April 11, just hours before Monroe arrived in Paris, Livingston met with Talleyrand. The French minister asked Livingston if the United States would like to buy the entire expanse of Louisiana.

The startled American replied that his country had no interest in land west of the Mississippi River, but merely wanted New Orleans and the Floridas.

11 The Louisiana Purchase

Dᴜʀɪɴɢ ᴀ ᴅɪɴɴᴇʀ ᴘᴀʀᴛʏ on April 12th celebrating Monroe's arrival at the American legation in Paris, Livingston was surprised to see Barbé-Marbois pacing about outside. A servant was sent to invite the Frenchman to join the diners for coffee. After pleasantries had been exchanged, Barbé-Marbois took Livingston aside and asked to meet him at the French treasury office later that night. They would discuss Napoleon's wishes regarding France's North American holdings.

Monroe wanted to accompany his colleague, but Livingston objected, using the trumped-up excuse that Monroe had no official powers because he had not yet been presented to Napoleon. Monroe was insulted and upset. Livingston seemed frantic about reaching an agreement with the French government by himself.

During the late-night meeting at Barbé-Marbois's office, the French minister told Livingston that Napoleon wanted to sell *all* of Louisiana. He counseled Livingston to hurry and purchase the vast North American territory because war was about to break out between France and Britain. When that occurred, he declared, England would attack New Orleans with its powerful navy, then troops would invade, occupy, and make the whole Mississippi Valley a British colony.

Nᴀᴘᴏʟᴇᴏɴ ᴅᴇᴄɪᴅᴇᴅ *to give up his dream of a North American empire and expand his power in Europe.*

As Bonaparte's official negotiator, Barbé-Marbois offered to sell the entire territory of Louisiana for $22,500,000.

Livingston believed he was being asked to buy half a continent. However, neither he nor Monroe had instructions or authority to do so. Despite this, he pursued the matter, replying that the amount asked for Louisiana was greatly beyond his country's means. Nevertheless, he "would be ready to purchase provided the sum was reduced to reasonable limits." Although reluctant to say so, he felt obligated to add that he would need to consult with Monroe before concluding negotiations.[1]

Livingston hurried home and worked until 3 o'clock in the morning composing a letter to Secretary of State James Madison. "I speak now without reflection & without having seen Mr. Munroe [sic] as it was midnight when I left the Treasury office. . . . It is so very important that you shd. be apprized that a negotiation is actually opened even before Mr. Munroe has been presented. . . . We shall do all we can to cheapen the purchase but my present sentiment is that we shall buy." The letter ended with the assurance that "Mr. Munroe would be presented to Marbois the next day," and would have "as early an audience as possible from the First Consul [Napoleon]."[2]

Livingston sent the letter as proof that he was arranging to buy Louisiana without the aid of Monroe. However, Livingston had no choice but to include Monroe in future conferences because Monroe ranked above him as America's official spokesman.

On April 15 the two Americans offered eight million dollars. Bonaparte cleverly pretended to have second thoughts about selling Louisiana unless much more money was offered.

For the next two weeks Monroe was confined to bed with agonizing backaches. Livingston kept negotiating without him.

On April 27 Livingston and Barbé-Marbois came to Monroe's apartment so that the ill envoy could participate. Napoleon had lowered his price to 16 million dollars.

Two days later, on April 29, Monroe felt well enough to go

with Livingston to Barbé-Marbois's office.

They countered with an offer of about 12 million dollars.

Astonishing Results

In the days before a telegraph or reports via steamship could speed communications, American diplomats in France were forced to act without consulting their government. Although operating beyond their authorized power, Livingston and Monroe finally agreed to pay 15 million dollars.

Defining the boundaries of Louisiana proved to be the most difficult part of the treaty. As Napoleon's spokesman, Barbé-Marbois was instructed to avoid delineating precise boundaries. The wording was so vague that the limits of the territory sold were open to a variety of interpretations. The boundaries were stated to be the same as they were when Spain possessed it.

What the United States was buying was not clear. Even though it was assumed that Louisiana extended to the Rockies, western borders were not defined. No one determined where the Spanish territories of Texas and New Mexico stopped and Louisiana began.[3] Eastern boundaries were not specified either. Since the Americans were sure that the Floridas were part of Louisiana, they were anxious to include a statement to that effect in the treaty. When informed that this territory still belonged to Spain, the two American envoys accepted a verbal promise from Barbé-Marbois that the French would put pressure on the Spanish so that the United States would eventually obtain this land.[4]

Financing the Purchase

The United States could not afford to pay 15 million dollars in cash. In 1803 the government had a national debt of $7,852,000 and was in no position to spend more money. Barbé-Marbois came to the rescue. He arranged for Alexander

Baring of Baring & Co., a British bank, to lend money to the United States.[5] Before lending the money, the bank asked the British Prime Minister for permission.

Even though England had declared war against France on May 18, 1803—16 days after the Louisiana Purchase Treaty was signed—the Prime Minister favored financing the deal to keep the French out of North America.

Napoleon sold Louisiana to the British bank for cash. The bank then turned ownership over to the United States in exchange for American bonds. These bonds were United States government promissory notes for borrowing money that would be paid back—plus 6 percent interest—in 15 years.[6]

Terms of the Treaty

One week before the treaty was signed, Napoleon issued a document that included the essentials to be included in the Louisiana Purchase agreement. He specified the following conditions:

■ *"Louisiana, its territory, and the dependencies appertaining thereto, shall become part of the American Union and shall constitute in due course one or several States according to the terms of the Constitution of the United States.*

■ *"The United States undertake to favor in a special way the commerce and navigation of French citizens. . . . Moreover, it is agreed that in the ports and towns of Louisiana, French and Spanish commerce shall enjoy perfect freedom to import goods. French and Spanish vessels and merchandise shall never be subjected to any of the customs or dues which may be imposed upon the commerce of other nations.*

■ *"Debts due to American citizens. . . shall be held to be canceled."*[7]

The Louisiana Purchase Treaty between the United States and the French Republic was based on this document.

IN THIS ARTIST'S RECREATION, *Livingston is signing the treaty and Monroe is shaking hands with Barbé-Marbois in front of a portrait of Louis XIV.*

It included Napoleon's demand that all of Louisiana be part of the United States and that its occupants enjoy the full rights of citizenship. Bonaparte made this demand because he did not want the vast area of Louisiana to be ruled as a colony that might one day be sold to another country. He also hoped to create a unified, more powerful United States that would be France's ally against England.

By April 30 agreements between the American envoys and Barbé-Marbois were drawn up. On May 1 Napoleon ratified a treaty with the United States, and on May 2 the papers were signed (although dated April 30).

The sale was Napoleon's decision.

Even though the American envoys had no authority to spend 15 million dollars or to purchase any land other than New Orleans and the Floridas, both Livingston and Monroe signed the treaty.

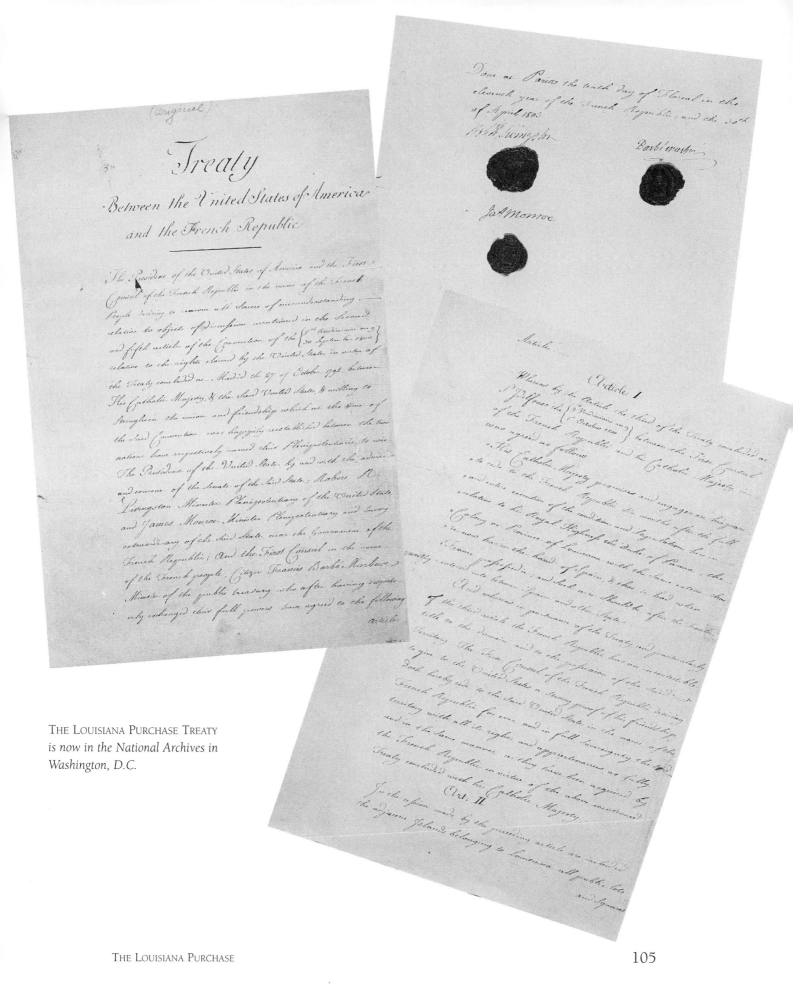

THE LOUISIANA PURCHASE TREATY
is now in the National Archives in
Washington, D.C.

12 Jefferson's "Empire of Liberty"

NEWS OF THE SALE arrived in the United States on July 3, just in time for President Jefferson to celebrate Independence Day with unrestrained elation. He had always envisioned an "empire of liberty" that encompassed western territory. He had predicted that the Mississippi River would become "one of the principal channels of future commerce for the country" and was confident that Louisiana's "fertile lands" would make America's economy flourish.[1] Now Lewis and Clark's "Voyage of Discovery" could openly send back reports about America's new Louisiana Territory.

Jefferson's dream of a peaceful westward expansion was becoming a reality!

An ecstatic Jefferson released the news to Washington's newspaper, the *National Intelligencer*, which heralded July 4 as a day of "widespread joy of millions at an event which history will record among the most splendid in our annals." It extolled the President for expanding the nation's holdings without resorting to war, saying that "truth and reason have been more powerful than the sword."[2]

THE U.S. CAPITOL BUILDING, *shown here in 1800, was the site of heated debates over the government's right to purchase Louisiana.*

The acquisition of new territory, however, did not please everyone. News that Livingston and Monroe had signed an agreement with Napoleon caused storms of protest from quite

a few Federalists. They were disturbed because instead of obtaining a river port and a small amount of territory, the American diplomats had spent millions for a vast area that was probably wasteland. And they were all too anxious to criticize and undermine Jefferson, their political opponent, who would be running for re-election in 1804.

East Coast newspapers fueled the flames of dissent by describing Louisiana as "a wilderness unpeopled with any beings except wolves and wandering Indians."[3] Reporters attacked the cost, pointing out that 15 million dollars was an enormous debt that might bankrupt the country. One writer described the money as the equivalent of 433 tons of silver, which would fill 866 wagons lined up for five and a half miles. Another newspaper told its readers that 15 million dollars' worth of silver dollars when piled up would be three miles high—enough to pay an army of 15,000 men 50 shillings a week for 25 years.

The Louisiana Purchase Treaty had to be approved by Congress before it became binding.

Jefferson's political opponents vehemently denounced the transaction because they feared that the new western members of the Union would take control of the government. They foresaw losing power to new states that would be created in an expanded West.

Delaware's Senator Samuel White declared that if the "howling wilderness," Louisiana, should ever be incorporated into the Union, it would be "the greatest curse that could at present befall us," that it would be "highly injurious and dangerous to the United States" because "we have already territory enough."[4] Connecticut's Senator Roger Griswold asserted that just as the government had no lawful right to annex England or France, it could not make the foreign territory of Louisiana part of the Union. Massachusetts's Senator Timothy Pickering railed against enriching the tyrant Napoleon and argued that

DISAPPROVAL *of the Louisiana Purchase is shown in this cartoon. A Federalist mocks Jefferson for coughing up millions of dollars to enrich the "hornet" Napoleon.*

Congress could not acquire new territory without "the assent of each individual state."[5] Massachusetts's Congressman Joseph Quincy was so violently opposed to the Purchase that he wanted the northeastern states to secede "amicably if they can; violently if they must."[6]

Despite these outcries of outrage, opposition was limited in scope. With the exception of some Easterners, most Americans shared the expansionist enthusiasm of Jefferson and were pleased about the Louisiana Purchase.

Was the Purchase Unconstitutional?

There could be a problem having the treaty approved by Congress, because the Constitution made no provision for acquiring new land and giving citizenship to inhabitants living outside the United States. Jefferson was deeply troubled by this. He admitted to a friend that the Purchase was "an act beyond the Constitution" and therefore he had no legal authority to sanction the Purchase.[7]

Nevertheless, he was determined that Congress accept the Louisiana Purchase Treaty. Even though he admitted that he had no constitutional authority to do so, he had to remove aggressive France from the continent to ensure the nation's security. If Napoleon controlled the interior of North America, he would be a dangerous enemy. The tyrant would destroy Jefferson's dream of

FEDERALISTS ACCUSED JEFFERSON of bowing down before the altar of France. In this cartoon he is stopped from burning the Constitution by the American eagle. The document labeled "Mazzei" refers to a letter Jefferson wrote attacking a Federalist leader.

an expanding America, needed for its growing population.

Should the treaty be blocked on legal grounds, Jefferson prepared a constitutional amendment that included this statement: "Louisiana, as ceded by France to the United States, is made part of the United States."[8]

On August 17th, the President read a letter from Livingston stating that "the consul [Napoleon] is less pleased with it [the treaty]. . . . In short he appears to wish the thing undone."[9] The letter warned that Napoleon would void the treaty if the American government made the slightest modification of its terms.

Jefferson knew that haste was crucial: Napoleon regretted the sale and was threatening to keep Louisiana. The French tyrant might trash the treaty unless it was ratified quickly.

The President realized that it would take a long time to amend the Constitution. Therefore, he overcame his queasiness about adhering to the Constitution strictly and advised Congress to act with as little debate as possible, "particularly so far as respects the constitutional difficulty."[10] Trusting that good sense would prevail, Jefferson submitted the treaty to the Senate.

The treaty was rushed through the Senate within four days and ratified by a vote of 24 to 7 on October 20, 1803.

Spain Protests

Spanish officials were outraged when they learned about the Purchase. Napoleon had betrayed them! The land belonged to Spain, not France. Bonaparte's troops still occupied the Kingdom of Etruria, and French officials still ruled there. That kingdom had not been exchanged for Louisiana. Therefore, since Bonaparte had not abided by the Treaty of San Ildefonso, France didn't own any part of mainland North America. And even if Napoleon had not cheated them by refusing to swap Etruria for Louisiana, the tyrant had broken his verbal promise never to sell the land unless Spain wished to buy it back.

Carlos Irujo, the Spanish Minister to the United States, exclaimed that the Americans were paying for stolen goods that rightly belonged to his country. He instructed officials in New Orleans to defend Louisiana. He dispatched agents to incite Indians against American settlers, and the Spanish government alerted its officials in Havana, Cuba, that they must prepare ships to blockade American ports.

Jefferson reacted by threatening to take Louisiana by force and attack the Floridas, too. Aware of its military inferiority, Spain backed down.

Spanish officials were instructed by King Charles IV to participate in formalities that transferred ownership to France. The French would then perform their own ceremony that would make Louisiana a territory of the United States.

13 America's Louisiana Territory

FRENCH COMMISSIONER PIERRE LAUSSAT had looked forward to becoming Governor of France's new North American empire. Much to his dismay, he learned that he would never have a chance to rule because Napoleon had sold the territory. He had been in New Orleans for months preparing for the French takeover from Spain. Laussat had hoped to be Governor for at least six or eight years. He anticipated that his wife and their three daughters would enjoy New Orleans, where "there is a great deal of social life; elegance and good breeding."[1]

He was not happy to learn that he had to participate in two transfer ceremonies.

Two Spanish grandees arrived from Madrid to participate in the first transfer ceremony on November 30, 1803. On New Orleans's main square, inside the government house—known as the Hôtel de Ville by the French—they placed the keys of the city's forts on a silver platter and presented them to Laussat. They then stepped onto a balcony overlooking a crowd to declare that the people of Louisiana were no longer subjects of the Spanish Crown. The only noise was that of cannon shot, made to herald the occasion. Spectators in the square were sullen and silent as they watched officials take down the Spanish flag and raise the French Tricolor in its stead.

PAINTED IN 1803, *this shows New Orleans as a prosperous port.*

On December 20, after France had possessed Louisiana only 20 days, a heartbroken Laussat appeared on the main balcony of the Hôtel de Ville facing the square. He was ready to surrender France's North American territory. At noon a 20-gun salute signaled that American soldiers had entered the city.

Two commissioners appointed by President Jefferson arrived. They were William Claiborne, Governor of Mississippi Territory, and James Wilkinson, Commanding General of the United States Army—but still Spain's paid secret Agent Number 13.[2] Claiborne and Wilkinson proceeded to the Hôtel de Ville. Laussat led them to the balcony, where he announced to the crowd below that Napoleon had authorized him to surrender the colony of Louisiana to the United States.

Governor Claiborne assured listeners that the Americans would receive them as brothers and that they would enjoy liberty and religious freedom.

The Tricolor of France came down, never again to wave on the continent of North America. The Stars and Stripes was raised. There were musket shots, salutes, hoorays from elated Americans, and sobs from distraught French people.

Laussat burst into tears and left the Hôtel de Ville hastily.

When President Jefferson received news of the transfer, he acknowledged it to be the greatest triumph of his political career. He hailed the purchase of his "empire of liberty" as "ample provision for our posterity and a widespread field for the blessings of freedom."[3] There were parties and celebrations all over the country, where people exclaimed that there had not been a comparable occasion for rejoicing since the adoption of the Constitution. A reporter for the *National Intelligencer* applauded President Jefferson's leadership by stating, "Never have mankind contemplated so vast and important an accession of empire by means so pacific and just."[4]

Jefferson had intended to buy New Orleans from France, and wound up acquiring all of Louisiana—an area approximately

WILLIAM CLAIBORNE *Governor of Mississippi Territory, attended the ceremony (right) in which France transferred Louisiana to the United States.*

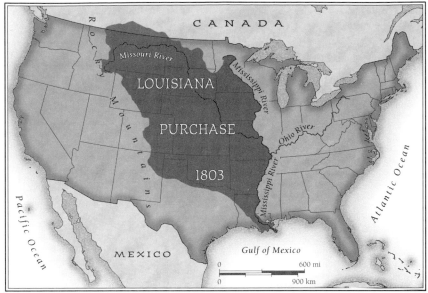

THE LOUISIANA PURCHASE *stretched from the Mississippi River to the Rocky Mountains and from Canada to the Gulf of Mexico.*

Present-day boundaries are shown.

one-third the size of the present 48 contiguous U.S. states. At the cost of about four cents an acre, the Louisiana Purchase doubled the size of the new nation. The government annexed an area of land larger than the combined size of present-day Spain, Portugal, Italy, France, Germany, the Netherlands, Switzerland, and Great Britain. Over time, all or parts of 15 states were created from the newly acquired Louisiana Territory: Arkansas, Colorado, Iowa, Kansas, Louisiana, Minnesota, Missouri, Montana, Nebraska, New Mexico, North Dakota, Oklahoma, South Dakota, Texas, and Wyoming.

Alarm, anxiety, and apprehension about having a foreign nation dominate the Mississippi Valley disappeared. Napoleon had jettisoned his plans for an empire in America. A new world to conquer was no longer his goal. He focused upon becoming master of Europe.[5]

The Louisiana Purchase was not inevitable.

The history of North America would have been different had Napoleon decided to keep Louisiana.

There could have been other outcomes.

■ This great conqueror, who declared that "peace is opposed to my interest," might have made Louisiana a well-populated French-speaking colony, aggressive enough to invade lands belonging to the United States, and powerful enough to claim regions that reached the Pacific.[6]

■ England might have declared war against France, conquered Louisiana, and made the territory a British colony.

■ The United States might have allied itself with England, declared war on France, and gained Louisiana for itself, or shared the land with the British.

■ Kentucky, Tennessee, and other states might have seceded from the Union rather than lose control of the Mississippi River. These states might have allied themselves with any foreign country that owned Louisiana or formed their own separate government and become a separate nation.

■ If Napoleon had deferred to Spanish objections about a broken treaty and let Spain continue to rule, the Spanish probably would have occupied Louisiana only until a mightier nation took the territory. English, French, and American forces were more powerful than Spanish troops.

Napoleon's decision to sell Louisiana and President Jefferson's decision to buy it shaped America's destiny. There were no longer reasons to fear that France or England or Spain would lay claim to the vast territory and then plot to invade the United States.

Instead, the Louisiana Purchase would transform the young United States from a weak nation, vulnerable to threats by foreign countries, into a great power respected throughout the world.

DROVES OF PIONEERS *headed West as a result of the Louisiana Purchase.*

Time Line

1682 La Salle claimed land he named Louisiana for France. It stretched from Canada to the Gulf of Mexico and encompassed unspecified territory east and west of the Mississippi River.

1754–1763 The French and Indian War, waged by England against France, was won by England.

1762 France secretly agreed to give Spain New Orleans and Louisiana west of the Mississippi River.

1763 According to the treaty of 1763 that ended the French and Indian War, England gained land in Canada and the area east of the Mississippi River (except New Orleans) from France. It also acquired the Floridas from Spain.

1766 Spain sent its first administrator to govern Louisiana.

1775–1783 The American Revolution was fought.

1783 The Treaty of Paris ended the American Revolution. England gave the United States all of its lands south of Canada, north of the Floridas, and east of the Mississippi River and returned the Floridas to Spain.

1784 Spain closed the Lower Mississippi River to foreigners.

1785–1789 Thomas Jefferson represented the United States in France.

1789–1797 George Washington served as President of the United States.

1789–1799 The French Revolution was fought.

1790–1793 Thomas Jefferson served as President Washington's Secretary of State.

1793 Citizen Edmond Charles Édouard Genêt recruited Americans to invade Louisiana and take it from Spain. His schemes were quashed, and he was dismissed as France's Minister to the United States. King Louis XVI and Queen Marie Antoinette were guillotined. President Washington issued a proclamation of neutrality.

1795 The Jay Treaty was signed. England agreed to evacuate her forts on United States Territory. The Pinckney Treaty was signed in which Spain accepted the 31st parallel as the north boundary of West Florida and agreed to give the United States free navigation rights on the Mississippi.

1797   France was ruled by the Directory, composed of five members. Napoleon, the hero of France, had been victorious in Italy and was successfully fighting in Austria.

1797–1800   The quasi war was waged between the United States and France.

1797–1801   John Adams served as President of the United States; Thomas Jefferson was his Vice President.

1799   Napoleon seized power and became France's dictator.

1800   The secret Treaty of San Ildefonso was signed. Spain agreed to give New Orleans and Louisiana west of the Mississippi River to France. Napoleon was supposed to give Spain the Kingdom of Etruria in return.

1801   Toussaint L'Ouverture, an ex-slave and dictator of St. Domingue (now Haiti), took control of the whole island of Santo Domingo (now Hispaniola). Robert Livingston, appointed by President Jefferson, became U.S. Minister to France.

1801–1809   Thomas Jefferson served as President of the United States.

1802   Spain's King Charles IV officially transferred Louisiana to France. Spain's administrator in New Orleans closed the port to American shipping. Napoleon declared himself consul for life.

1802–1803 Napoleon sent troops to St. Domingue. The French were defeated.

1803 James Monroe was named Envoy Extraordinary to France by Jefferson so that he could help Livingston negotiate with Napoleon. Jefferson planned the Lewis and Clark expedition. The Louisiana Purchase Treaty was signed by Livingston, Monroe, and Barbé-Marbois. Through President Jefferson's efforts, the treaty was ratified by Congress.

AFTER THE PURCHASE TREATY *was ratified, the Lewis and Clark expedition crossed America's Louisiana Territory and proceeded west to the Pacific Ocean. This illustration shows the explorers on the Columbia River.*

C A N

Missouri River

MONTANA
1889

NORTH DAKOTA
1889

LOUISIANA

SOUTH DAKOTA
1889

WYOMING
1890

NEBRASKA
1867

PURCHASE

COLORADO
1876

KANSAS
1861

1803

OKLAHOMA
1907

NEW MEXICO
1912

TEXAS
1845

Pacific Ocean

MEXICO

Present-day boundaries are shown.

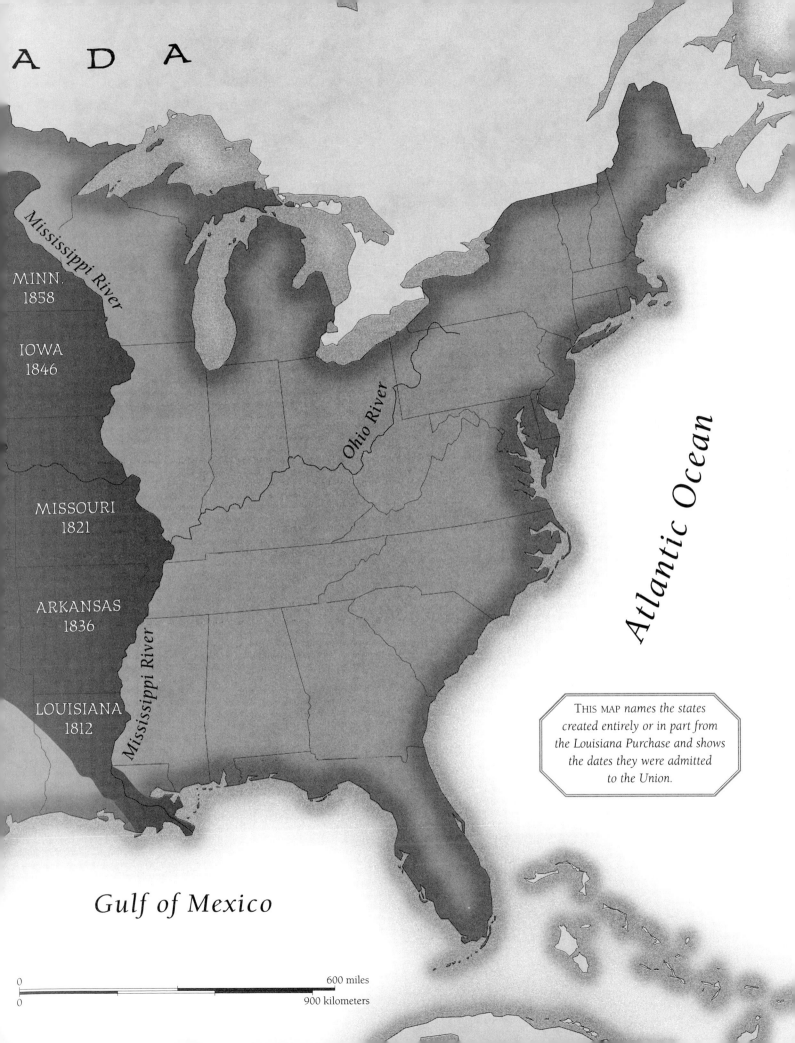

A D A

MINN.
1858

IOWA
1846

MISSOURI
1821

ARKANSAS
1836

LOUISIANA
1812

Mississippi River

Ohio River

Mississippi River

Atlantic Ocean

Gulf of Mexico

THIS MAP *names the states
created entirely or in part from
the Louisiana Purchase and shows
the dates they were admitted
to the Union.*

0   600 miles
0   900 kilometers

Notes

Chapter 1: Napoleon Eyes North America

1. Marshall Sprague, *So Vast, So Beautiful a Land,* p. 4.

2. Anka Muhlstein, *La Salle,* p. 157.

3. Alexander DeConde, *This Affair of Louisiana,* p. 10.

4. E. Wilson Lyon, *Louisiana in French Diplomacy,* p. 32.

5. Hodding Carter, *Lower Mississippi,* p. 48.

Chapter 2: Spanish Louisiana

1. *The Paris Treaty of 1783* (University of Oklahoma Law Center via the Internet).

France, America's staunchest ally, did not ask for territory in North America.

Chapter 3: American Settlers

1. Willard Randall, *Thomas Jefferson,* p. 522.

2. Merrill Jensen, The New Nation, p.172.

3. In 1791 Wilkinson became a lieutenant colonel in the United States Army. In 1796 he became General in Supreme

Command of the United States Army, a position he held until 1812. He was on the Spanish payroll until 1803 or 1804. In 1805 he became Governor of Louisiana Territory!

4. Roger G. Kennedy, *Orders from France,* p. 306.

5. Alexander DeConde, *This Affair of Louisiana,* p. 52.

Chapter 4: A French Conspiracy

1. Alexander DeConde, *This Affair of Louisiana,* p. 79.

2. Marshall Sprague, *So Vast, So Beautiful a Land,* p. 250.

3. Genêt was forced to drop his grandiose schemes. As an enemy of a new set of rulers in France, his life would have been in danger had he returned to his country. President Washington showed compassion for this obnoxious, insolent ex-minister. He granted him political asylum in the United States. Genêt became an American citizen, married the daughter of New York's wealthy Governor George Clinton, enjoyed life devoid of politics, and retired to raise a family and preside over a Long Island duck farm.

Chapter 5: Avoiding War

1. Pro-British Federalists and Pro-French Republicans had surfaced when Hamilton was Washington's Secretary of the Treasury and Jefferson was Secretary of State. As chief officers with opposing views on foreign policies, they found themselves "daily pitted in the cabinet like two cocks": Hamilton praising the British government as "the best in the world," Jefferson expressing his devotion to France. However, political parties were not organized until 1794, the year Federalist John Jay was commissioned to make a treaty with England. (Margaret C. S. Christman, *"The Spirit of Party,"* p. 14.)

2. Henry Steele Commager and Milton Cantor, *Documents of American History,* Volume I, "The Jay Treaty," p. 165.

3. Arthur B. Darling, *Our Rising Empire,* p. 218.

4. Roger G. Kennedy, *Orders from France,* p. 158.

5. *Ibid.,* p. 49.

6. Alexander DeConde, *The Quasi-War,* p. 68.

7. Philadelphia was the capital of the United States from 1790 to 1800.

8. To demonstrate his pro-American feelings, Napoleon ordered ten days of national mourning when he learned that George Washington had died in December 1799. As a true admirer of the former President, he decreed that a bust of Washington be placed in the Grand Gallery alongside those of other historic heroes, such as Hannibal and Caesar. It was in this climate of good will that Napoleon cordially greeted the American envoys.

Chapter 6: A Tyrant's Treaty

1. "Memoirs of the Queen of Etruria," published in *Memoirs,* by Baron de Kolli, p. 309.

2. *Ibid.,* p. 310.

3. Napoleon annexed Etruria to his empire in 1807.

4. "Memoirs of the Queen of Etruria," p. 320.

5. *Ibid.,* pp. 339, 331.

Chapter 7: The "Black Napoleon"

1. The French owned two other islands in the West Indies: Guadeloupe and Martinique. These were not as valuable as St. Domingue.

2. Roger G. Kennedy, *Orders from France,* p. 131.

3. Charles Tansill, *The United States and Santo Domingo,* p. 34.

4. In 1801 President Thomas Jefferson worried that Toussaint's successful emancipation of blacks could incite insurrections in America. Consequently, he informed the French minister in Washington that ". . . nothing would be easier than [for the United States] to furnish. . . [the French] army and fleet with everything, and to reduce Toussaint to starvation." (Henry Adams, *History of the United States, 1801–1809,* p. 279.) Jefferson wanted to help Napoleon oust the black dictator. It did not occur to him that Bonaparte intended to use St. Domingue as a supply center for French conquests on mainland North America. After defeating Toussaint, it would not be long before French soldiers occupied the Mississippi Valley and became a threat to the United States.

5. At this time the whole island was called Santo Domingo (now Hispaniola). The French colony of St. Domingue occupied the western part of the island. The eastern part of the island (now the Dominican Republic) belonged to Spain.

6. Henry Adams, *History of the United States, 1801–1809,* p. 279.

7. Wenda Parkinson, *"This Gilded African,"* p. 168.

8. *Ibid.,* p. 280.

9. Henry Adams, *History of the United States, 1801–1809,* p. 264.

Chapter 8: Jefferson's Minister to France

1. Willard Randall, *Thomas Jefferson,* p. 565.

2. Livingston, New York's most prominent landowner, was one of the most fascinating men of his time. Like Jefferson, he enjoyed a passionate interest in an incredible variety of subjects. He read every book that came his way, including those about soil conservation, water purification, stock breeding, and

farming. Through experimentations on his own farm, he attempted to increase the yield of wheat, corn, and clover. To improve breeds of cattle, he tried the impossible: unsuccessfully mating his cows with an elk. He studied clouds and weather patterns, planned to supply New York City with "pure and wholesome" water, made paper from riverweed, and hoped to develop a steamboat that would enhance trade and transportation on the Hudson River. Jefferson considered his friend's ideas brilliant.

The President's fondness for Livingston was fired by the constant intellectual stimulus they provided for each other. It relieved their preoccupations with politics. How diverting and delightful it was for the just-inaugurated President Jefferson to read Livingston's long letter about fossils. It described three teeth of a prehistoric animal that may have been "shaped either like a Baboon or a bear." The letter also contained comments about mammoths, other extinct species, and the possible evolution of new species. [This in 1801, 55 years before Darwin's theory of evolution!] (George Dangerfield, *Chancellor Robert R. Livingston of New York,* p. 297.)

3. *Ibid.,* p. 309.

4. Henry Adams, *History of the United States, 1801–1809,* p. 276.

5. *Ibid.,* p. 311.

6. James Hosmer, *The History of the Louisiana Purchase,* p. 122.

7. E. Wilson Lyon, *Louisiana in French Diplomacy,* pp. 161, 162.

8. Arthur B. Darling, *Our Rising Empire,* p. 429.

9. Henry Steele Commager and Milton Cantor, *Documents of American History,* Volume I, "Letter to Robert R. Livingston, April 18, 1802," p. 109.

Many historians believe that Jefferson sent this letter as a ploy, knowing it would be read by French intelligence agents, and that the President had no intention of an alliance with England.

10. Alexander DeConde, *This Affair of Louisiana*, p. 103.

11. George Dangerfield, *Chancellor Robert R. Livingston of New York*, pp. 331–335; Lyon, pp. 159–161.

Chapter 9: A National Crisis

1. Although a preliminary agreement had taken place in October 1800, the Spanish had refused to sign official papers until 1802. Even though the Kingdom of Etruria had not been handed over to them, they accepted Napoleon's promise that he would not sell Louisiana to another foreign nation.

2. Robert Tallant, *The Louisiana Purchase*, p. 71.

3. Alexander DeConde, *This Affair of Louisiana*, p. 121.

4. *Ibid.*, p. 127.

5. James Hosmer, *The History of the Louisiana Purchase*, p. 62.

6. Willard Randall, *Thomas Jefferson*, p. 566.

7. Arthur Whitaker, *The Mississippi Question: 1795–1803*, p. 208.

8. Harry Ammon, *James Monroe: The Quest for National Identity*, p. 204.

9. *Ibid.*, p.207.

10. *Ibid.*, p.206.

11. Jefferson, *Message to Congress* (via the Internet).

12. Alexander DeConde, *This Affair of Louisiana*, p. 103.

Chapter 10: Napoleon Changes His Mind

1. According to Harry Ammon, Talleyrand, Lucien, and Joseph were offered enormous bribes if they could persuade Napoleon to keep the peace (Ammon, *James Monroe*, p. 209). Other sources do not mention that Lucien was offered a bribe from the British.

2. François de Barbé-Marbois, *The History of Louisiana*, p. 264.

3. Marshall Sprague, *So Vast, So Beautiful a Land*, p. 302.

Chapter 11: The Louisiana Purchase

1. "Letter from Livingston to Madison, April 13, 1803," *American Heritage*, April 1955, p. 28.

2. *Ibid.*, p. 29.

The misspelling of Monroe as "Munroe" appeared in the letter.

3. Texas became a state in 1845; New Mexico became a state in 1912.

4. The United States did not obtain the Floridas until 1819.

5. Baring & Co. was sure that backing the United States promised profits. In 1795 Alexander Baring, a son of the firm's leading partner, had been sent to the United States to appraise three million acres in Maine. The land was owned by one of the wealthiest men in the country, Senator William Bingham of Pennsylvania. Alexander Baring not only purchased one million acres from the Senator (at 33 cents an acre), he also married one of Bingham's daughters!

Through financial and family contacts, Alexander Baring invested heavily in United States bonds and businesses. It was not surprising, therefore, that this banker backed the prospect of American expansion. He deserves credit for expediting the Louisiana Purchase.

6. Hope and Company of Amsterdam was another bank that helped finance the sale. Based on Alexander Baring's judgment, it took 40 percent of the deal.

Bonaparte was so elated by the role played by Barbé-Marbois that he gave his minister a gift of 192,000 francs—money used by Marbois as a dowry for his daughter. (E. Wilson Lyon, *The Man Who Sold Louisiana*, p. 123.)

7. "Napoleon's Order for the Sale of Louisiana, April 23, 1803," translation of document found in James Hosmer, *The History of the Louisiana Purchase*, Appendix B, p. 214.

Chapter 12: Jefferson's "Empire of Liberty"

1. Thomas Jefferson, *Notes on the State of Virginia*, pp. 7, 166.

2. Alexander DeConde, *This Affair of Louisiana*, p. 178.

3. *Ibid.*, p. 178.

4. *The Annals of America, Volume 4 1797–1820*, p. 175.

5. DeConde, p. 190.

6. "Louisiana Purchase," *Compton's Encyclopedia Online*.

7. *The Annals of America*, p.172.

8. *Ibid.*, p. 173.

9. George Dangerfield, *Chancellor Robert R. Livingston of New York*, p. 134.

10. *Ibid.*, p. 174.

Chapter 13: America's Louisiana Territory

1. Pierre Clément de Laussat, *Memoirs of My Life*, p. 119.
He praised New Orleans because the city had ". . . all sorts of masters—dancing, music, art, and fencing, etc. . . . no book shops or libraries, but books are ordered from France."

2. Shortly after the ceremony, Wilkinson received money from Spain for services he would render in the future. He advised Spanish authorities to fortify Texas and Florida frontiers against American attack, to maintain control over the neighboring Indians, and to stop the explorations headed by Lewis and Clark. Fortunately, they were unable to catch up with the Lewis and Clark expedition.

3. Willard Randall, *Thomas Jefferson*, p. 567.

4. Dumas Malone, *Jefferson and His Time*, Volume 4, p. 338.

5. Napoleon proceeded to conquer most of Europe. His troops were finally stopped in Russia because of bitter winter weather. He was crowned Emperor of France in 1804 but lost his throne in 1814. A return to power after being exiled on the island of Elba lasted one hundred days. Napoleon was defeated in Belgium at Waterloo in 1815 and was banished to the island of St. Helena, where he died in 1821.

6. Lucien Bonaparte, *Memoirs*, p. 307.

Bibliography

Primary Sources

———. *American History Told by Contemporaries, Volume III, National Expansion: 1783–1845.* Macmillan Co., 1896:

> Bonaparte, Lucien, "How Napoleon Persisted in Selling Louisiana."
> United States Senators, "Objections to Annexation (1803)."
> Inhabitants of Louisiana, "Petition for Representative Government."

Barbé-Marbois, François de. *The History of Louisiana.* Reprint of 1830 edition, Baton Rouge: Louisiana State University Press, 1977.

Bonaparte, Lucien. *Memoirs.* New York: Harper & Bros., 1836.

Commager, Henry Steele, and Milton Cantor. *Documents of American History.* Volume I. Englewood Cliffs, New Jersey: Prentice-Hall, 1988:

> "The Jay Treaty"

"The Pinckney Treaty"

"Jefferson on the Importance of New Orleans (Letter to Robert R. Livingston, April 18, 1802)"

"The Cession of Louisiana, April 30, 1803"

Jefferson, Thomas. *Notes on the State of Virginia*. Chapel Hill: University of North Carolina Press, 1955.

Laussat, Pierre Clément de. *Memoirs of My Life*. Reprint of 1803 edition, translated by Sister Agnes-Josephine Pastwa. Baton Rouge: Louisiana State University Press, 1978.

"Letter from Livingston to Madison, April 13, 1803," *American Heritage*. April 1995, pp. 26–29.

"Memoirs of the Queen of Etruria," published in *Memoirs of My Life,* by Baron de Kolli. London: Treuttel and Würtz, 1823.

"Memoir of Livingston Addressed to Talleyrand Feb. 1, 1803," *Annals of Congress, 1802–1803,* pp.1078–83 (from Hosmer, James. *The History of the Louisiana Purchase*. Appendix A p. 205).

Monroe, James. *Autobiography*. Edited by Stuart Brown. Syracuse, New York: Syracuse University Press, 1959.

"Napoleon's Order for Sale of Louisiana, April 23, 1803" (from Hosmer, James. *The History of the Louisiana Purchase*. Appendix B, p. 214).

"Treaty of Purchase between the United States and the French Republic (April 30, 1803)," *Annals of Congress, 1802–1803,* pp. 1006–1008 (from Hosmer, James. *The History of the Louisiana Purchase*. Appendix A, p. 205).

Secondary Sources

———.*The Annals of America Volume 4: 1797–1820*. William Benton, publisher. Chicago: Encyclopaedia Britannica, 1900.

Adams, Henry. *History of the United States, 1801–1809*. New York: The Library of America, 1986.

Ammon, Harry. *The Genêt Mission*. New York: Norton & Co., 1973.

———. *James Monroe: The Quest for National Identity*. New York: McGraw-Hill, 1971.

Carter, Hodding. *Lower Mississippi*. New York: Farrar & Rinehart, Inc., 1942.

Christman, Margaret C. S. *"The Spirit of Party": Hamilton & Jefferson at Odds*. Washington, D.C.: National Portrait Gallery, 1992.

Cresson, W. P. *James Monroe*. Chapel Hill: University of North Carolina Press, 1946.

Dangerfield, George. *Chancellor Robert R. Livingston of New York*. New York: Harcourt, Brace and Co., 1960.

Darling, Arthur B. *Our Rising Empire*. Seattle: Archon Books, 1962.

DeConde, Alexander. *This Affair of Louisiana*. New York: Charles Scribner's Sons, 1976.

————. *The Quasi-War.* New York: Charles Scribner's Sons, 1966.

Foley, William. *The Genesis of Missouri.* Columbia: University of Missouri Press, 1989.

Hoobler, Thomas, and Dorothy Hoobler. *Toussaint L'Ouverture.* New York: Chelsea House, 1989.

Hosmer, James. *The History of the Louisiana Purchase.* New York: D. Appleton and Co., 1902.

Jensen, Merrill. *The New Nation.* New York: Alfred A. Knopf, 1962.

Kennedy, Roger G. *Orders from France.* New York: Alfred A. Knopf, 1939.

King, Grace. *New Orleans: The Place and the People.* New York: Macmillan Co., 1899.

Lyon, E. Wilson. *Louisiana in French Diplomacy.* Norman: University of Oklahoma, 1934.

————. *The Man Who Sold Louisiana.* Norman: University of Oklahoma, 1942.

Malone, Dumas. *Jefferson and His Time.* Volumes 2–4. Boston: Little Brown and Co., 1951, 1962, 1970.

Muhlstein, Anka. *La Salle, Explorer of the North American Frontier.* New York: Arcade Publishing, 1994.

Parkinson, Wenda. *"This Gilded African" Toussaint L'Ouverture.* London: Quartet Books, 1978.

Perkins, Bradford. *The Cambridge History of American Foreign Relations.* Volume 1. Cambridge, England: Cambridge University Press, 1993.

Randall, Willard. *Thomas Jefferson.* New York: Henry Holt & Co., 1993.

Ronda, James, ed. *Thomas Jefferson and the Changing West.* St. Louis: Missouri Historical Society Press, 1997.

Sprague, Marshall. *So Vast, So Beautiful a Land.* Boston: Little, Brown & Co., 1974.

Tallant, Robert. *The Louisiana Purchase.* New York: Random House, 1952.

Tansill, Charles. *The United States and Santo Domingo, 1798–1873.* Baltimore: The Johns Hopkins Press, 1938.

Tucker, Robert, and David Hendrickson. *Empire of Liberty.* Oxford, England: Oxford University Press, 1991.

Whitaker, Arthur. *The Mississippi Question: 1795–1803.* Gloucester, Mass.: Peter Smith, 1962.

Ziegler, Philip. *The Sixth Great Power.* New York: Alfred A. Knopf, 1988.

Illustrations Credits

Rhoda Blumberg used the following sources to obtain period illustrations:

pp. 16, 22, 30, 33, 39, 41, 45, 51 (all), 53, 62, 65–68, 73–75, 77, 82–84, 88 (both), 92–95, 107, 114–15, Reproduced from the collections of the Library of Congress; pp. 17, 27, 61, 70–72, 76, Courtesy Biblioteque Nationale de France; p. 18 (upper), "La Salle Claiming Louisiana for France. April 9, 1682," by George Catlin, Paul Mellon Collection, photograph © 1998 Board of Trustees, National Gallery of Art, Washington, D.C.; pp. 18 (bottom), 49, 52, 64, 81, 89–90, Courtesy New York Public Library; pp. 20–21, Courtesy Walters Art Gallery, Baltimore, Maryland; pp. 23, 56, Courtesy Museo del Prado; pp. 24, 25, 28, 36–37, 55, 80, 103, 112, Courtesy Tulane University Library; p. 31, "Old Ste. Genevieve," by O. E. Beringhaus, courtesy State of Missouri; p. 32, Courtesy Missouri Historical Society; pp. 34–35, 44, Courtesy Peabody Essex Museum, Salem, Massachusetts; pp. 36, 43, Courtesy Independence National Historical Park Collection; pp. 46–47, Courtesy U.S. Naval Academy Museum; p. 54, Courtesy Huntington Library, San Marino, California; p. 63, Courtesy Schomburg Collection, New York Public Library; p. 86, Courtesy Collection of the City of New York; p. 105 (all), James E. Russell NGP; p. 109, Joseph H. Bailey NGP; p. 110, Courtesy American Antiquarian Society; 118–119, "Westward the Course of Empire Takes Its Way," courtesy Bancroft Library, University of California, Berkeley; p. 123, "Lewis and Clark on the Lower Columbia," by Charles M. Russell, courtesy Amon Carter Museum, Fort Worth, Texas.

Index

Illustrations are indicated by **boldface**. If illustrations are included within a page span, the entire span is boldface. Material in the Notes has been indexed, with the page number and note number (n) given.

Rhoda Blumberg has been acclaimed for her masterful presentations of landmark events in history. She won the 1997 *Washington Post*-Children's Book Guild Award for her overall contribution to nonfiction for children. *School Library Journal* says that the author "shines in the imaginative use of extensive research to tell, compellingly and entertainingly, stories from history."

Rhoda Blumberg and her husband, Gerald, live in Yorktown Heights, New York.